LUNDY PACKETS

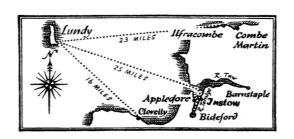

. . . sometimes you may see the grey mass of Lundy, on the horizon.
Lonely Lundy, to which His Majesty's mails go only once weekly from
Instow Quay, per sailing-skiff Gannet. For those who like the tumbling of
the ocean wave, the cruise there and back in the day on those weekly
sailings is enjoyable; but for those who do not happen to be good sailors,
the return fare of five shillings only admits to five shillings' worth of
sheer misery. So Lundy generally remains to unseaworthy visitors to
Instow a great unknown quantity.

CHARLES HARPER, *THE NORTH DEVON COAST*, 1908

LUNDY
PACKETS

BY
MIKE TEDSTONE

TWELVEHEADS PRESS

TRURO 2001

CONTENTS

TWELVEHEADS PRESS

First published 2001 by Twelveheads Press.
Chy Mengleth, Twelveheads, Truro, Cornwall TR4 8SN.
ISBN 0 906294 47 9
British Library Cataloguing-in-Publication Data.
A catalogue record for this book is available from the British Library.
Designed by Alan Kittridge. Printed by The Amadeus Press Ltd., Cleckheaton, West Yorkshire.

INTRODUCTION

A long, low wall of purple on the horizon . . .
P. H. GOSSE

Where is Lundy? It sits out in the Bristol Channel, between Wales and Devon, and marks a boundary where the Channel opens out and becomes part of the Atlantic. Lundy has a strong presence all its own and is neither Welsh nor particularly English in character, existing independently. Not really belonging to anywhere else by association, one's perception of Lundy from the mainland is shaped by its inaccessibility set against its visibility, at least from the nearer coast of North Devon. If this Severn Sea, beginning as the River Severn on the slopes of Plynlimon in Wales, has an ending then Lundy sits astride that point, a remote and evocative shape on the horizon with a somewhat forbidding appearance.

For the mariner, under sail, Lundy represented either somewhere to be avoided in adverse winds or, alternatively, a safe haven in a westerly gale. From the vantage point of Lundy the views on a clear day are immense, as Devon gives way to Cornwall on the one hand and on the other, Gower links to West Wales in the far distance. But, for early excursion steamer passengers, the perspective from up-Channel was quite different, where Lundy represented the *Ultima Thule* of destinations, being near-exotic to trippers from Cardiff, and most certainly in a wholly different category from the relatively mundane charms of Mumbles or Weston-super-Mare.

Lundy Island, pictured from a departing steamer, on the Bristol Channel side.
ALAN KITTRIDGE

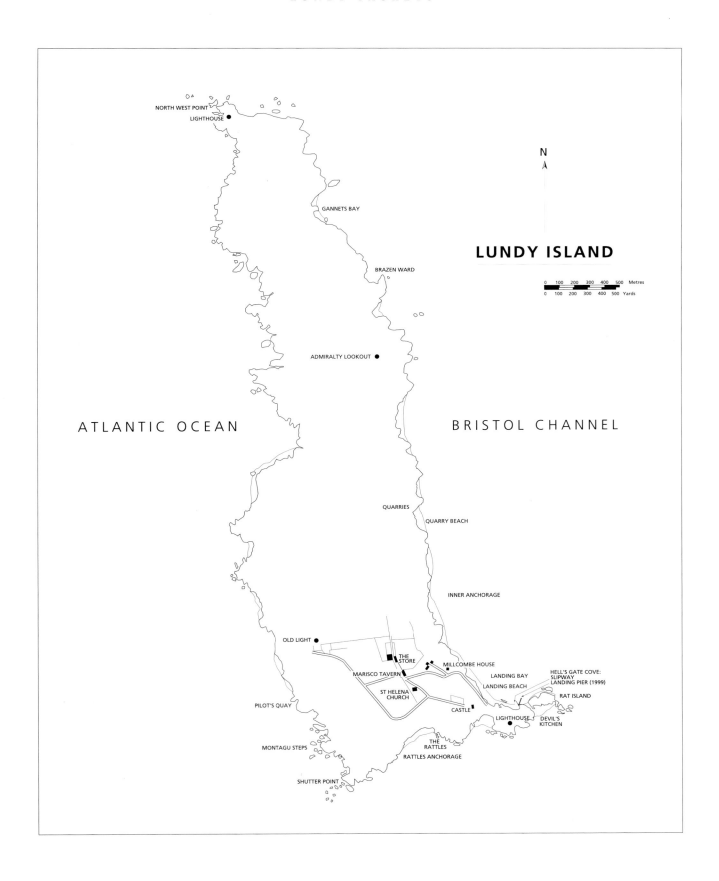

NORTH WEST POINT
LIGHTHOUSE ●

N

GANNETS BAY

BRAZEN WARD

LUNDY ISLAND

0 100 200 300 400 500 Metres
0 100 200 300 400 500 Yards

ADMIRALTY LOOKOUT ●

ATLANTIC OCEAN

BRISTOL CHANNEL

QUARRIES

QUARRY BEACH

INNER ANCHORAGE

OLD LIGHT ●

THE STORE

MILLCOMBE HOUSE

MARISCO TAVERN

LANDING BAY

HELL'S GATE COVE:
SLIPWAY
LANDING PIER (1999)

ST HELENA CHURCH

LANDING BEACH

RAT ISLAND

PILOT'S QUAY

CASTLE

LIGHTHOUSE ●

DEVIL'S KITCHEN

MONTAGU STEPS

THE RATTLES

RATTLES ANCHORAGE

SHUTTER POINT

In the nineteenth century J. R. Chanter gave possibly the most succinct description of the location of the island, only a little over three miles long by a mile wide. He referred to its unique character, and linked it firmly to the nearer shores of England, about twelve miles distant from craggy Hartland Point in Devon. His words described the image perfectly:

In the Bristol Channel, nearly facing the centre of Barnstaple Bay, but above twenty miles from the Bar, and almost in mid-Channel, lies the island of Lundy, sometimes invisible from the shore, but generally looming dim and mysterious, and more or less shrouded in mists, or capped with cloud-reefs, occasionally standing out lofty, clear, and distinct, bright with varied hues of rock, fern, and heather, its granite cliffs glittering as they reflect the rays of the morning sun, and the graceful lighthouse tower and buildings plainly defined; or at night traceable by its strange intermittent light - either suddenly shining out as a star and as suddenly vanishing, or gradually rising and fading, according to the atmospheric conditions; but in all aspects, varying much from day to day.

Over the centuries Lundy has had numerous owners, each with different intentions. A move away from earlier piratical practices had taken place by the 1830s when William Hudson Heaven acquired the island for his own residence, and fortunately much is documented of the many and varied aspects of Lundy after this threshold. Our starting point is around the middle of the nineteenth century, shortly before regular communications between Lundy and the mainland commenced to satisfy the needs of the Heaven family. There is very little evidence surviving of the handful of minor vessels that served Lundy spasmodically before W. H. Heaven entered into what was to become a lasting contractual relationship with Captain Dark of Instow, but the purpose of this book is to document the succession of the six principal Lundy mailboats, commencing with the sailing boat *Gannet* which was followed by the steam coaster *Devonia*. Then followed two fishing vessels, the long-lived *Lerina* and subsequently *Lundy Gannet*. In the 1970s the coaster *Polar Bear* took over and now, after an extensive refit in 1999, the motor vessel *Oldenburg* has

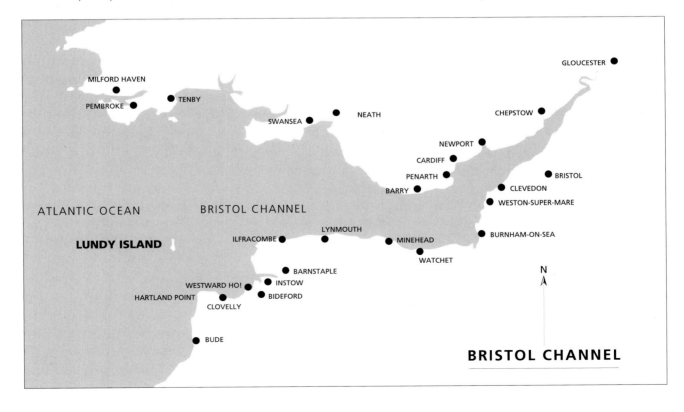

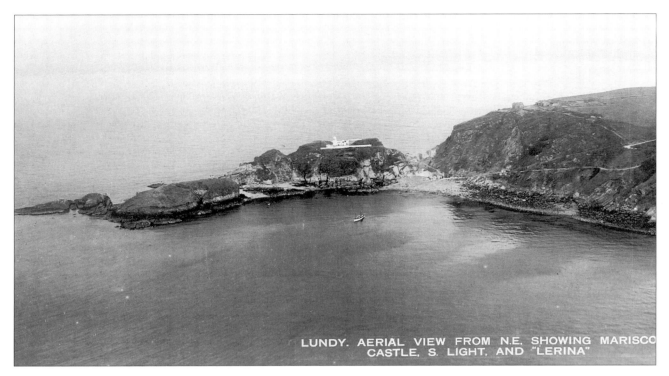

LUNDY. AERIAL VIEW FROM N.E. SHOWING MARISCO CASTLE, S. LIGHT, AND "LERINA"

A view of the landing beach showing Marisco Castle, South Light and the Lundy Packet LERINA. TOM BAKER COLLECTION

possibly brought about the greatest transformation ever to island-controlled services, and seems set for a long term role serving Lundy.

These are defined as the Lundy Packets, but a number of considerations underpin this succession. An important one is the impact of the development of postal services to Lundy on the vessels employed, and I have also endeavoured to record chronologically the 'secondary' vessels which have also been used to carry the mails and island supplies for whatever reason, as well as make reference to air services which have on occasions supplemented or substituted for sea transport. Also mentioned are the mainland ports used by the Lundy Packets over the years, as well as the various changes of ownership of Lundy that have taken place, and which have clearly impacted upon the shipping services. Another factor has been the relationship with the seasonal excursion steamer services, operated by a variety of companies, as these carried a large proportion of Lundy's visitors but were a quite separate business activity to that of dealing with the mail and cargo requirements of the island.

The history of the Lundy Packets is not particularly straightforward, but it might be observed that the needs of the small island have never been onerous as regards shipping, in terms of export traffic and a population which has rarely exceeded more than a few dozen. Lundy does, however, have immense charm, and has grown in popularity over the period covered by this book. After the island has grown from a distant faint outline to a looming and atmospheric, slightly forbidding and seemingly impregnable rocky fortress, much of the character of the voyage to Lundy has stemmed from landing at the island by small boat, and the attendant unpredictability associated with the restricted nature of the beach in certain weather conditions. But this has seen a fundamental change, with the opening in August 1999 of a new pier, and an excursion nowadays on the newly-refurbished *Oldenburg* is a very different experience to that which travellers endured in the nineteenth century and the larger part of the twentieth century, when journeying by sail or steam and landing by launch or dinghy - weather and circumstances permitting.

The image one retains of a summer voyage to Lundy is an appealing and exciting one, combining the beautiful coastal scenery of North Devon which, as it recedes astern, is replaced ahead by the gradually increasing bulk of the looming east side of Lundy with its four-hundred foot high cliffs. The near total absence of cars on the island now has just as strong an attraction as over sixty years ago when guidebooks could cheerfully refer to Lundy as being free of '. . . rates, taxes, policemen and motor-dust . . .' whilst accurately describing the sea-battered coastline as wild and dangerous. Highlights of scenery on the island are equally of a grand and wild nature with sheer precipices and pinnacled cliffs, yet ultimate tranquillity is there to be found too, on a calm day when Lundy '. . . shimmers in the heat encircled by a silver sunlit sea, with its drowsy silence broken only by the call of the birds and the lap of the waves . . .'.

My motive in writing this book derives from a most memorable first visit to Lundy on the White Funnel vessel *Balmoral* in 1976, and a number of subsequent visits including one by the ill-fated *Prince Ivanhoe* in 1981. Often, when ashore at Ilfracombe on Bristol Channel cruises, I used to see *Polar Bear* high and dry on her sheltered berth, and admire her chunky lines and distinctive whale-backed bow, but somehow the opportunity never arose to sail on her. Soon after *Oldenburg* had arrived at Bideford in 1986 I sampled her, and had the perfect weekend staying in the tranquil luxury of Millcombe, wholly captivated by the charms of the island. Whilst researching the background of the excursion vessels which have served Lundy over the past

century or so (for an article which appeared in the journal *Ships Monthly* in 1991), it seemed to me that the packet story warranted further investigation, as only the sketchiest references to the mailboats could be found, and I felt that more detail could usefully be assembled.

Perhaps the greatest joy has been to delve into the primary source material documenting the vessels within the Custom House Registers of Shipping covering the ports of Barnstaple, Bideford and elsewhere, and to see in copper-plate handwriting the very first entry for *Gannet*, back in 1878 when she was registered by Captain Dark of Instow. As there are no company records as such for Lundy, information has been garnered from a variety of sources, and I could not have put this story together without access to the Heaven diaries covering the early years. Much of the story of the *Devonia* interlude came from Post Office archive material, as this was a period when mail-contract and related issues virtually dictated the course of Lundy's shipping service. Equally important as a source is the autobiography of Felix Gade, *My Life on Lundy*, which I have used extensively to piece together the story of the two vessels associated with the period from 1926 to 1972 when Mr Gade was Lundy agent, namely *Lerina* and *Lundy Gannet*. A step-change on Lundy came with the end of private ownership in 1969 and the island's administration by the Landmark Trust, which brought into service first *Polar Bear* and then *Oldenburg*. These ships and the transformation brought about by the new pier, opened in 1999, are better documented in such sources as the *Illustrated Lundy News* and various Lundy Field Society publications.

CHAPTER ONE

BEGINNINGS

So at length we stowed ourselves in the sternsheets; the peak was hoisted, the jib was set, the mainsail trimmed; another pull upon the peak-halyards, the jib and main sheets tautened, and here we were with the red sails as flat as a pancake, facing the westerly breeze, and pitching and rolling in the wash of the sea, which is always more than ordinarily uproarious off the harbour's mouth just at the turn of the tide.

P. H. GOSSE

Although the cutter *Gannet* of 1878 has been chosen here as the first dedicated Lundy Packet, there were other vessels which served the island during the earlier years of the Heaven era. William Hudson Heaven, born in 1799, evidently chartered a variety of vessels to serve his needs, often from Clovelly, and the opening quote of this chapter is a description by Gosse, from his book *Land and Sea*, of a voyage from Ilfracombe to Lundy in an (unnamed) open boat as a guest of Hudson Grosett Heaven, the eldest son of W. H. Heaven, who was born in 1826.

Inevitably, W. H. Heaven would have needed to engage someone contractually to

look after the needs of his family when resident on the island, for supplies and communications before any form of telegraph system was installed. Trinity House shared the contract with Heaven until they employed their own contractor in 1871. Before there was any suggestion of an organised Post Office presence on Lundy, the arrangements for mails to and from the island reflected the differing interests and needs of the Heaven family themselves, Trinity House on account of the lighthouse and its personnel and, briefly during the 1860-70s, the Lundy Granite Company had a significant presence, and mail for employees of that organisation is known to

Agricultural implements being landed on Lundy from a sailing-vessel beached at low tide.
MYRTLE TERNSTROM
COLLECTION

THE HARBOUR, INSTOW.   2847

have passed by the company's own vessel, the *Vanderbyl* – named after one of the Directors of the Lundy Granite Co.

The period during which the Granite Company was active on Lundy was comparatively brief, 1863 to 1868, and little is known of their vessels. However, the Heaven diaries were kept by Amelia Heaven, daughter of W. H. Heaven, from 1870 onwards, and as a result there exists a skeletal record of the highlights of daily life on Lundy from the privileged perspective of one of the immediate family, which makes occasional reference to shipping movements, and from which one can infer how traffic patterns evolved.

At the point that the diaries commence, a Mr Bragge was contracted to the Heaven family and his skiff *Ranger* was deployed for the crossing from the mainland to Lundy. After Bragge had terminated his contract with the Heaven family, at Michaelmas 1871, he continued to service Trinity House, and his vessel *Chance* connected Lundy with Appledore. This service is believed to have operated at fortnightly intervals, and was taken over after Bragge's retirement in 1877

by a Mr Cox, and ran independently of Heaven family needs, well into the early part of the twentieth century. Old Devon guide books of the period make it clear that passengers could travel to Lundy from Appledore by this service if they wished.

The name Dark appears with greater frequency in the Heaven diaries after 1871, when he was sub-contracted by a Mr Fishwick to run a weekly service to and from the island. Mr Fishwick had initially used the fore and aft rigged *Mary*, but after this vessel was lost in 1872 the smack *Muffy* was briefly substituted before Captain William Dark took over in his own right using the trawler *Chase*. The service provided by Captain Dark was a weekly summer link (fortnightly in winter) between the little Torridge harbour at Instow and Lundy, and its commencement marked the beginning of a long family relationship with the island in the provision of the vital link with the outside world. Captain Dark thus handled the Heaven family mails *via* the Post Office at Instow, a conveniently short distance from Instow Quay, with Instow railway station close at hand.

A postcard view of Instow, Appledore and the River Torridge. The port of Appledore is to the extreme left of the picture (on the west bank of the Torridge), and the steps of Instow Quay are clearly visible in the middle. In the foreground at the water's edge is the Southern Railway line at Instow station, connecting Barnstaple on the River Taw (from the right-hand side of the picture) and Bideford, up-river on the Torridge, behind the photographer. Directly behind Instow Quay lies Braunton Burrows. Lundy lies out of sight, to westwards. Instow Post-Office, where the Lundy mails were handled, is situated approximately midway along the waterfront between the Quay and the railway station. Author's collection

Very basic early landing-stage arrangements on the beach at Lundy, nineteenth-century. The paddle-steamer VELINDRA, moored offshore, was based at Swansea and ran seasonally to Lundy.
MYRTLE TERNSTROM
COLLECTION

Perusal of the Heaven diaries often highlights the difficulties then experienced in depending on sailing-craft to carry the mails, in terms of the number of occasions when the weather might impose disruption, and often three or even four weeks might go by but no mailboat would arrive at Lundy. Then, during a lull, perhaps Captain Dark would appear unexpectedly and deliver the long-awaited mailbag, and a flurry of activity would ensue as letters were answered in the brief period before he had to return to catch the tide to make it safely back over the Bideford Bar. But whilst *Chase* carried out its regular, seemingly mundane role, numerous other vessels might appear off Lundy, and the opportunity would be taken by the family to induce a ships captain to carry some urgent item of mail to whatever mainland port might be possible.

Excursion steamers were also a factor by this time, albeit often in the shape of passenger-carrying tugs prior to the advent of purpose built vessels. Pockett of Swansea was the most prominent company insofar as Lundy was involved, and their paddle-steamer *Velindra* – which might be regarded as the first excursion steamer of any consequence to visit Lundy regularly each summer – is recorded as first having carried out a Lundy excursion in June 1869. Prior to this, Pockett's smaller *Prince of Wales* is on record as having offered the occasional Lundy excursion in between her regular Swansea to Ilfracombe packet sailings: that finally advertised for Thursday 23 August 1860 had been postponed twice that month on account of 'the inclement and unseasonable weather' according to the Ilfracombe newspaper *Bright's Intelligencer and Arrival List*. Elsewhere in this journal, in

September 1860, is recorded an account of an individual's delightful day trip from Clovelly to Lundy styled as 'The Rambles of a Vagabond in North Devon', the passage to and from the island being achieved by the simple expedient of chartering an idle pilot-cutter, in glorious conditions on this particular occasion. It should however be noted that Lundy was regarded very much as private property by its owner, and excursion steamers were tolerated rather than welcomed, Pockett being granted the rights annually by Mr Heaven. There was clearly little one could do to physically prevent people coming ashore in connection with pilot-cutter movements on Lundy. The P. & A. Campbell Ltd. steamers started to feature in the Bristol Channel in the 1890s, after the debut in 1887 of *Waverley*, although Lundy was not properly within their sphere of operations until much later. It might thus be argued that the Lundy Packets story really starts in the 1870s, with the Dark family connection becoming prominent after 1878 when the first packet vessel serving Lundy regularly entered service, the famous *Gannet*.

It is of interest that although the steamboat era had arrived by that time, transport by sailing boat was all that was deemed necessary for Lundy well into the early part of the twentieth century. The needs of the Heaven family were economically catered for by basically weekly sailings. For family members or guests coming and going to Lundy this service was effectively supplemented during the summer season by use of the excursion steamers. *Velindra* was then running on a weekly basis or occasionally twice-weekly, and less subject to the vagaries of the weather. On Monday 14 March 1870 Ann Mary Heaven (a niece of W. H. Heaven) was detained at Clovelly for four days whilst awaiting passage in *Ranger*. If one did not always have to wait so long for favourable conditions, it was just as likely that having once set off from the mainland the voyage by open boat could become protracted; on Friday 1 April 1870 the Heaven diary recorded that Bragge came in the morning, having set out the day before, on Thursday morning, at 6 o'clock.

The landing stage at Lundy.
DAVID TAPSELL COLLECTION

On Thursday 9 June 1870 Amelia Heaven recorded that everybody was watching for the skiff in the morning, but it did not arrive until 7 p.m. Such irregularity was of great significance to the family as their affairs would partly depend on being able to respond to newly-arrived letters by return, whilst the mailboat waited in the bay, rather than not be

Pockett's Bristol   *Steam Packet*
Channel   Co. *(Ltd.)*

MARINE EXCURSIONS
FROM ILFRACOMBE
PER THE SALOON PASSENGER STEAMSHIP

VELINDRA

Weather and other circumstances permitting.
The only Excursion Steamer in the Bristol Channel
Classed A-1 Lloyds.

WEDNESDAY, August 16th, at 10-15 a.m.,

To CLOVELLY,
Returning at 4 p.m.
Steamer Leaves for Swansea at 6 p.m.

THURSDAY, August 17th, at 3 p.m.,

CHANNEL TRIP
Steamer leaves for Swansea at 7 p.m.

FRIDAY, August 18th, at 10.15 a.m.,

To LUNDY ISLAND
Returning at 4 p.m.
Steamer Leaves for Swansea at 6 p.m.

SATURDAY, August 19th, at 10.45 a.m.,

TO CLOVELLY,
Returning at 4 p.m.
Steamer leaves for Swansea at 6 p.m.

FARES (including landing and embarking):—
To Clovelly and back, Best Cabin, 3s. 6d.; Fore Cabin, 2s. 6d. Single to or from, 3s. To Lundy Island and back, Best Cabin, 3s. 6d.; Fore Cabin, 2s. 6d. To Lynmouth and back, 3s. 6d.; Single to or from, 2s. 6d. Channel Trip, Best Cabin, 1s. 6d; Fore Cabin, 1s. To Swansea, Best Cabin, 4s. 6d; Fore Cabin 3s. 6d.

Tickets at the Office on the Pier. Refreshments can be obtained on board, and at the Stores on Lundy Island.

Advertisement from the Ilfracombe Observer & North Devon Review, 15 August 1893.

A pre 1892 view of the landing beach from the sea.
HEAVEN ARCHIVE

Velindra, which would usually cross from Swansea to Ilfracombe on four or five days a week and then offer a variety of cruises from Ilfracombe to either Clovelly, Lundy (often on Tuesdays), Lynmouth or other North Devon coastal attractions. In 1870 visits by the excursion steamers *Thames* and *Prince of Wales* are recorded, the latter being in service from 1855 onwards. Visits by the smaller steamers *Digby Grand* and *Lord Stanley* are recorded in 1871, as well as *Spicy* which evidently brought a band over to play on Lundy on Monday 3 July 1871. There were even trips recorded by an early *Balmoral* in 1877.

One excursion operator, a Mr Rosser, started to trade from Ilfracombe in 1876 with the paddle-steamer *Flying Cloud*, seemingly in direct competition with *Velindra*. A wide range of destinations was offered by *Flying Cloud* including Westward Ho! which then had its shortlived pier. At least one documented visit to Lundy took place, on Wednesday 12 July 1876, but it appears that 'Rosser's Marine Excursions' ceased during August 1876.

By 1877 ownership of Lundy by the Heaven family had been established for over forty years, and transport arrangements between the mainland and the island simply reflected the needs of residents with the addition of seasonal influxes of day-trippers or, occasionally, guests of the Heaven family who would normally be accommodated at Millcombe, the dignified residence of the owner. But W. H. Heaven was by now an elderly man, and, after a serious bout of illness during the winter of 1875-6, which left him partially paralysed, his eldest son, the Revd Hudson Grosett Heaven (who had been the Headmaster of Taunton College School, but had returned to Lundy to live in 1863 after the school became insolvent) took charge of island affairs. This was to coincide with the establishment of a more formalised relationship with Captain William Dark, which enabled the latter to procure a newly built vessel with which he would tend to the Heaven family needs through a relationship that was to endure (at a later stage through his son Fred Dark) until 1918, when the island was sold out of the ownership of the Heavens after almost a century.

able to get a reply back to a mainland destination until a week had elapsed. Equally, the mailboat might come inconveniently early, depending on tides and weather conditions. On Sunday 7 April 1872 Mr Fishwick caused consternation and 'disturbed the peaceful slumbers of the household' by arriving early in the morning and departing again before breakfast. Dependability must have been highly prized, and one suspects that Captain Dark was seen as capable of providing this quality to the Heaven family. Aside from the comings and goings of the sailing-boats, instances were recorded in 1870 where both *Ogmore* and *Vanderbyl*, the Lundy Granite Company steamers, took letters to the mainland to be posted.

The sole documented reference in the diaries to *Muffy* was on Sunday 16 March 1873 when that vessel came 'to everyone's surprise. Nothing but letters and one or two parcels were landed'. Thereafter, references to Dark's vessel *Chase* become more frequent, for example on Wednesday 19 November 1873 when it was 'too rough to anchor in the bay so only a few things besides saturated letters were landed'. The erratic influence of the wind on landing conditions at Lundy was an omnipresent theme as, for example, on Saturday 20 March 1875 when, after *Chase* had anchored, the wind blew from the north-east 'and so only part of the cargo was landed and Dark hastily retreated'.

The variety of excursion vessels calling in this period is notable, apart from the almost regular visits of the substantial 'Pockett Packet'

CHAPTER TWO

GANNET
THE EARLY YEARS

And the Gannet is a fine seaworthy craft, commanded, too, by as handsome a son of North Devon as you will find between Glenthorne and Marsland – a skipper tall and straight and sunburnt, with brown beard and clear blue eye that has looked a roaring sou-wester square in the face many a time between Bideford Bar and Lundy. The Gannet sails from Instow every Thursday with the mails . . .
J. L. WARDEN PAGE

The Custom House Register for the Port of Barnstaple records that *Gannet* was first registered jointly in 1878 in the names of William Dark of Instow, Master Mariner, and Alfred Thomas Powell of Instow, Gentleman, each holding half of the 64 shares in the vessel. Exactly how Captain Dark identified this vessel as suitable for carrying out his Lundy contract for the Heaven family remains the subject of speculation, but when interviewed by a *Lloyds News* reporter in 1911 shortly before his retirement, he stated that *Gannet* had been laid down with the intention of becoming a Cherbourg pilot-boat, but that he purchased her from the Swansea yard of G. B. Meager 'off the stocks' having decided that she would be just what the Lundy trade needed. Describing the beginnings of his involvement with Lundy, Captain Dark recalled that when he originally started his service he had a cutter, the *Chase*, built and that vessel was succeeded by a tug-boat, the *Advance*. Before running to Lundy to service the Heavens' needs, Captain Dark had been in the employment of the Lundy Granite Company.

The details of *Gannet* as recorded in the Barnstaple Register of Shipping were as follows:

No.	72443
Port	Barnstaple
Port no.	3/1878
Built	British-built
Type	Sailing Ship
Where built	Swansea, G. B. Meager & Co., 1878
Description	One deck, one mast, smack-rigged, square-stern

Tonnage	19.02 gross registered tons
Build	Carvel, galley-none, head-none, framework-wood
Length	44.9 ft.
Breadth	13.1 ft.
Depth	6 ft 5.5 ins. (in hold from tonnage deck to ceiling at midships)

Little evidence of shipbuilding in the Port of Swansea remains today, but it was a significant activity in the early part of the nineteenth century, with a partnership between William Meager & Richards on record from around 1812 to 1840, based

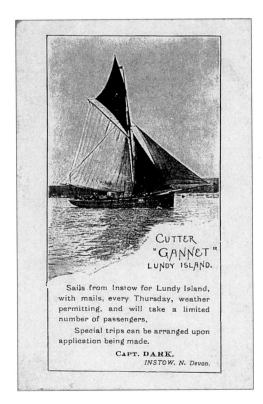

CUTTER "GANNET" LUNDY ISLAND.

Sails from Instow for Lundy Island, with mails, every Thursday, weather permitting, and will take a limited number of passengers,

Special trips can be arranged upon application being made.

CAPT. DARK.
INSTOW. N. Devon.

Capt William Dark's business card.
TOM BAKER COLLECTION

The cutter GANNET, *built at Swansea in 1878. Photographs of her are scarce, and in this superbly evocative view one would guess that Captain Dark was making ready to depart from Lundy for the mainland on one of his weekly crossings, during the period late nineteenth century to possibly as late as around 1916.*
TOM BAKER COLLECTION

initially at the Phoenix dry dock. George Blaney Meager, the grandson of the first William Meager, built the Villiers dry-dock in 1852, which typically could handle vessels of up to about 500 tons. The most active days of Swansea wooden shipbuilding were apparently between the late 1850s and the early 1870s, but the arrival of steamships seemingly caused the diminution of this activity. No trace of these docks remains today, but George Owen of Swansea recalls seeing them in derelict condition in the 1920s. It is not known whether *Gannet* was built in the Villiers dry-dock or simply on a slip, but it seems reasonable to suppose that her name was chosen for the new trade once Captain Dark assumed ownership. The link between Captain Dark of Instow (a native of Clovelly, but resident in the Torridge port) and Swansea is not as tenuous as it might seem today, as trading links across the Bristol Channel were well established then, for example by Pocketts of Swansea which traded from the 1850s onwards between Swansea, Wadebridge, Padstow and as far afield as Bristol offering packet and cargo services. Local interests at Bideford were involved in the packet link between that port and Bristol.

The new cutter *Gannet* settled down easily to her duties, and the Heaven diaries first record her arriving at Lundy on Thursday 27 June 1878. This was an occasion of some moment for the island, and unusual in that the new packet-boat stayed overnight. The diary entry for this occasion records:

> Wind, South-East. Warm, but very strong for a hot summer day. Millie at cottages after dinner. Annie bathed before, went later to beach where Mr. Dovell was shooting mullet (got one after). Dark's new boat (Gannet) came, Mrs. Dark and cousin thereby, and two new serving maidens Mary Jane Davis and M. I. White. Everyone from cottages down for letters. Thirteen eggs, three Houduns. Thunder and Lightning. Friday 28th. Wind South-West, rain and more wind, and more distant thunder and more coldness. Gannet went. Velindra came, about 20 passengers.

Captain Dark had interests in a number of vessels at that time, and occasional mentions of

The steam-tug ADVANCE, pictured alongside at Bideford Quay, was briefly in the part-ownership of Captain William Dark and is recorded in the Heaven diaries as having made occasional Lundy trips in 1884 and 1885.
MEDINA GALLERY, BIDEFORD

his *Chance* servicing Lundy are made until 1884, as well as calls by the steam tug *Advance* in 1884 and 1885. The Shipping Register records that the co-owner of *Gannet*, Mr A. T. Powell, sold his half-share to Captain Dark on 14 November 1881, and one infers that his business was prospering at that time for such a transaction to be feasible. Charter or other trips to Lundy, or elsewhere, were also advertised by Dark at this time, outside the Heaven contractual requirements.

As regards the mail service, there was still no Post Office presence on the island and as *Gannet* conveyed the Heaven family mails and general supplies to and from Instow Post Office, no particular contractual relationship with the Post Office was necessary. However, this situation was not to last, and the age of the principal members of the family provides a pointer to developments in the mid-1880s. W. H. Heaven (the Squire) died in 1883, but his son (the Revd) – who had been in charge of island affairs since 1876 – was then almost sixty years old. Mr Wright, a lessee, arrived in 1885 and took over the farm and stores, the year in which the Revd H. G. Heaven fulfilled his ambition to build a church on Lundy, a pre-fabricated iron structure at the top of Millcombe. The need to import building materials for this church possibly explains the use of more vessels than simply relying on the limited capacity which *Gannet* could provide, although it had been the custom to charter

QUEEN OF THE BAY, *pictured at the opening of the floating dock, Penzance in 1884. Two years later she was employed carrying mail to Lundy.*
ROYAL INSTITUTION OF CORNWALL

special boats for heavy cargoes – coal, cattle, etc. – usually 'Pengelby's boat'.

Mr Wright predictably felt the need to make changes after his installation on the island, and the next phase of mailboat activity derived from his wish to have a more organised link by steamboat as well as the setting up of a Post Office and his appointment, in 1887, as sub postmaster. One particularly notable diary entry of the time described Wright as being 'wrath with Dark' – we might wonder just what irregularity induced this sentiment! The vessel chosen to carry out this duty, *Queen of the Bay* built in 1867 by Henderson, Colbourn & Co. of Renfrew, had an interesting history, including a lengthy spell as a Penzance to Isles of Scilly packet boat before going to Cardiff. She was employed by the Post Office as a packet-boat and it is clear from advertisements in the *Western Mail* newspaper that she was not regularly participating in the growing Cardiff excursion steamer trade, but was generally offered for charter duties by her owner, John Dutton.

Heaven diary references at this time give glimpses of what was happening on Lundy – on 10 May 1884 the Revd Heaven sent his first telegram by the newly installed submarine cable which linked the island with Hartland Point. The telegraph office was manned daily by employees of Lloyds of London, who monitored shipping movements in the channel. On Tuesday 6 January 1885

frustration with Captain Dark's services was tersely recorded thus: 'Dark came in steamer . . . poor man seems out of spirits the horrid tug charged £20 for towing him out the other day'. The first evidence of imminent change to the weather-dependent mailboat sailings offered by *Gannet* is to be found in the diary entry for Wednesday 21 April 1886 where Mr Wright, having arrived with Captain Dark, brought tidings that the Government had agreed to a weekly postal link with Cardiff, using a tugboat on Wednesdays. It was established that a sub post-office would be set up at the store, but it was noted that a weekly arrival from Cardiff with immediate return of the vessel would not permit letters to be answered on the same day, clearly a retrograde step from the Heaven family viewpoint. On Wednesday 30 June 1886 it is recorded that the steamer *Queen of the Bay* came to Lundy, and that her owner Mr Dutton came up to Millcombe to ask for leave for a few passengers to be landed – which was granted just for that occasion.

The commitment to run a steamship at weekly intervals all the way from Cardiff to Lundy for the postal needs of the modest island population could scarcely be seen as other than a somewhat unlikely business proposition, and the diaries make it clear that the comings and goings of *Gannet* were not altered by the introduction, from 3 March 1887, of this new steamboat-operated packet service and the Heaven family mails continued to travel with Captain Dark in the accustomed manner under sail *via* Instow.

The paddle-steamer *Queen of the Bay* had originally seen service as an excursion steamer in the Morecambe and Blackpool areas, transferring to the ownership of the West Cornwall Steamship Company in 1874, who had her reboiled by Harvey's of Hayle the following year. She was sold to John Dutton of Cardiff in November 1885. Farr records that she ran some Cardiff Ilfracombe trips in 1883, and had a passenger certificate for 138 in the Home Trade and 197 for excursions. She was in Dutton's ownership until December 1889, before changing hands a couple of times and eventually was burnt in the River Usk in May 1894, finally being sold as a wreck.

It is not stated in the Heaven diaries whether *Queen of the Bay* was viewed as a particularly unreliable vessel in herself, but the picture one gathers from all the entries recording her mail sailings to the island during the 1887-8 period is an erratic one, with arrivals occasionally at odd times, or sometimes with the wrong mailbags. Post Office officials came to Lundy in August 1887 to check personally on alleged irregularities in the service, and on one occasion in November that year the mail delivered to the island had already been a week on board the steamer, according to the scandalised diarist! In early 1888 two other vessels are recorded as having brought the Cardiff mails instead of *Queen of the Bay*. These were *Clarissa* and *Lord Derby*, both seemingly minor non-passenger carrying vessels. By early-1888 it had become apparent that the Cardiff mail steamer arrangement was not going to continue, the most telling diary entry being that of 20 April 1888 stating that 'Dark has Government postal employ . . . is to bring mails every Thursday without prejudice to our day'.

The last Cardiff mail sailing took place on Friday 4 May 1888. On the same day Captain Dark is recorded as having brought Government Mail, for the first time. *Gannet* thus became the first dedicated Post Office

packet as well as the principal mail and supplies link with the mainland, and the pattern of the basic weekly connection resumed, subject to the vagaries of the weather. Captain Cox continued to attend to the Trinity House interests with his twice-monthly service from Clovelly. To complete the passenger shipping picture at this point it only requires reiterating that *Velindra* would still run her weekly or twice-weekly excursions to Lundy from Ilfracombe, normally between May and September. The soon-to-be ubiquitous White Funnel – initially in the form of the Campbell-owned paddler *Waverley* – had also arrived in the Bristol Channel. Other passenger vessels mentioned in the Diary were Pockett's iron screw steamer *Rio Formoso* on Friday 21 September 1888 in lieu of *Velindra* which had broken down, and the paddle-tug *Privateer* on an excursion from 'over the Bar' (i.e. Bideford) on Thursday 23 August 1888.

Specific references to mailboat matters in the Heaven diaries became fewer once the situation with Captain Dark had consolidated after the relative excitement of the establishment of Lundy's post office, and its associated steamboat foray. Pockett's 'new' excursion steamer *Brighton* made her first appearances in the summer of 1894, and was soon to supersede the by-now elderly *Velindra*

GANNET, with fish-curing seemingly taking place on board. The appearance of Fred Dark (in trilby), centre, suggests the date of this photograph as being turn of the century. Surprisingly, this view was actually a postcard.
DIANA KEAST COLLECTION

in the Swansea Ilfracombe excursion trade. On 5 January 1895 it was recorded that 'Dark came to Rattles', a cryptic way of saying that weather conditions had made the landing-beach untenable and that one of the alternative landing-places had been used, in this case Rattles at the south of the island, causing extra difficulty. A number of other locations occasionally featured in at least getting the mail ashore from *Gannet*, such as Pilots Quay to the west of the island and (at a later stage) the Montagu Steps, to the southwest. Unusually, between the beginning of April 1896 and the end of May 1896, the diary recorded eight successive Thursdays where 'Dark came' normally, without disruption or diversion.

In the 1890s, then, the situation regarding passenger access to Lundy Island was quite straightforward – one either travelled in the summer season by paddle-steamer from Ilfracombe or Clovelly, or braved the rigours

Captain William Dark.
MYRTLE TERNSTROM
COLLECTION

of an open-boat crossing from the River Torridge if willing to take a risk on the weather, with the distinct possibility of landing on the island by an undignified scramble up rocks if an easterly made the landing beach unuseable. The Heaven family were quite content with this arrangement, even if other residents felt better facilities for passengers were warranted. Writing in the *Hartland Chronicle* in October 1916 the Revd B. Babington alleged that the Revd Heaven had positively resisted the construction of a pier or landing stage on his island as he did not want to make it too convenient for visitors as he was concerned at the damage caused to shrubs and flowers. Motivated by the fact that his wife had once fallen into the sea from Dark's small boat when attempting to land on Lundy, the Revd Babington (who had spent some time ministering on Lundy, and felt able to speak out publicly with some authority) claimed that the islanders did want better facilities, either in the form of a groyne or breakwater at least. However, when interviewed by a *Western Mail* reporter in 1906, shortly before he removed from Lundy finally to retirement on the mainland, the Revd Heaven made it clear that the intrusion from tourists had not been wanted by his family nor by Wright, even though a landing-stage may have been a feasible proposition – if it could have been afforded.

The *Thorough Guide to North Devon and North Cornwall*, published in 1892, featured a chapter on Lundy Island and had this to say about communications with the mainland, albeit not entirely accurately as regards the tonnage of *Gannet*:

Approaches The only fixed services are (i) Gannet (40 tons), on Thursdays, from Instow, at hours varying with the tide. The voyage, about 25 miles, takes 3 hours, and the skiff remains about 5 hours at the island. Single fare, 5s.; return, 7s 6d. Captain Dark (Primrose Cottage, Instow) has made this trip for many years, and on other than maildays the Gannet can be hired, to Lundy and back, for 30s. (ii) The Trinity House skiff from Appledore on the 1st and 15th of the month.

Perhaps the relationship of Captain Dark, his cutter *Gannet* and the Heaven family of Lundy could have continued indefinitely into the twentieth century, but a couple of events in the 1890s were to eventually lead to changes to the mailboat arrangements. The first was the formation, in 1894, of the Bideford and Bristol Steam Ship Company and the introduction into regular packet service between those two ports of the purpose-built coastal screw steamer *Devonia*. The second was the change in regime on the island which occurred in 1899, when a Mr Taylor took on the tenancy of the island, and the Heaven diaries record a certain amount of his comings and goings by means of that steamer from April 1899 onwards, rather than by *Gannet*. These calls at the island by *Devonia* were exceptional rather than routine, but were generally fitted in with her basic weekly schedule of sailing outwards from Bideford to Bristol on Mondays and returning down-Channel on Wednesdays. Mr Taylor had ambitions for the island, and whilst the now elderly Revd H. G. Heaven and his family remained resident at Millcombe with a reserved portion of the island, to all intents and purposes the rest was in Taylor's hands.

The *Hartland Chronicle*, in March 1899, noted that Mr G. J. Taylor of Abbotsham Court had 'entered into the possession of Lundy Island, the valuation having been made. In addition to farming it, he proposes making it a pleasure resort'. A *Bideford Gazette* item, also published in March 1899, went further and claimed that it was intended (by George Taylor) that *Devonia* would in the season make '. . . two calls weekly at Lundy for and with passengers and goods. It is expected that the journey will take about two hours and a quarter, which is a consideration when compared with the time taken by the sailing vessel now running. Hope is also expressed that Mr Taylor will provide accommodation for landing on the island . . .'. However, there was little immediate evidence of these expansionist aims although some years later, in March 1906, another fascinating *Hartland Chronicle* piece described great plans for new pleasure steamer services from Bideford to Lundy, linking in with trains to Bideford from

An undated view of GANNET *in the River Torridge*
TOM BAKER COLLECTION

the surrounding areas of North Devon. It was claimed that Mr Taylor had reached an understanding with the Directors of the Barry & Bristol Channel Steamship Company to operate their Red Funnel Line steamers on regular excursions in the summer season, and the paddle steamers *Gwalia*, *Devonia* and *Westonia*, which had started running in 1905, were named as the vessels that would provide this new facility, combined with greatly improved landing arrangements at Lundy. Needless to say this ambitious plan did not come to fruition, and in the early years of the twentieth century it remained the case that basically only the Pockett steamer *Brighton* operated Lundy excursion sailings.

Judging by some of the 1899 diary entries Mr Taylor might well have been unimpressed by the reliance on *Gannet*. On Friday 29 September 1899 Dark was 'driven back by a thunderstorm'. He came again on Saturday 14 October 1899 but did not anchor, although he managed to land two rams and some oats. Unable to wait for the mailbag, he did just manage to ship the Heaven family mailbox. On Thursday 19 October 1899 he came again, and finally managed to land some of the cargo which by then had been on board for some three weeks awaiting suitable conditions for discharge.

Conversely, on 27th June 1900 it was recorded that *Gannet* was 'just flopping about in the calm' and so a tug-boat was asked to give her a tow. In the meantime numerous instances of *Devonia* acting in a general cargo role continued to be recorded, often shipping consignments of cattle. Amelia Heaven died on 26 October 1905 and the diary ceased shortly before this, but the very last entry concerning *Gannet* makes one marvel at how that small open vessel and its three-man crew coped, as on 5 September that year some 35 ewes were shipped to the island.

Although *Gannet* was to go on to serve as Lundy's supply boat for many more years, her mailboat days were now numbered, and ironically she gave up that role because of the failure of Captain Dark to agree new terms with the Post Office after he had an engine installed in her in 1911, in an attempt to improve reliability. Before moving on to the period where *Devonia* took over the mailboat role in 1911, it should be mentioned that one of Lundy's most notable shipwrecks occurred in 1906 when HMS *Montagu* struck. Aside from the magnitude of the loss to the Royal Navy caused by this well-documented event, its practical effect was to put the hitherto little-known island well and truly on the map.

Immediately after HMS *Montagu* struck excursion steamers flocked to Lundy with passengers eager to view the wreck and the subsequent attempts to recover the ship ran on for several years, having become the subject of extensive national media attention. Although a first 'one-off' White Funnel call at Lundy had taken place in 1898, when *Lady Margaret* brought across a bell-ringing party from Ilfracombe by arrangement to ring in the bells of the then newly-completed church of St Helena, no regular pattern of Lundy calls by the White Funnel Fleet had been established prior to the HMS *Montagu* wreck in 1906, nor by their competitors the Red Funnel Line. The two companies each put a different slant on their excursions to view the wrecked ship, which were offered virtually daily by both operators right until the September of that year; the non-landing White Funnel Fleet trips were described as 'Special Cruises to view wreck of HMS Montagu at Lundy Island'. Intriguingly, the management of the Red Funnel Line must have negotiated with the

Revd Heaven, who was then said to be about to sell up and leave Lundy permanently to retire to his home in Somerset, and offered a cash inducement to persuade him to overcome his dislike of visitors, as their sailings were billed as 'Special Trips to Lundy Island (to land), the Scene of the Stranded Battleship Montagu'.

A toehold in Lundy excursion sailings was thus first established by the Red Funnel Line and later by P. & A. Campbell Ltd. in 1910 and the frequency of Lundy calls began to gradually increase each year thereafter. It was perhaps no coincidence that the Revd Heaven finally gave up full-time residence on Lundy that year to live on the mainland in his old age, returning only in successive summers.

Charles G. Harper, who wrote a number of finely-observed books about the West of England and its coastal scenery at this time, gave an evocative picture of Lundy in the 1908 edition of *The North Devon Coast*, having acidly commented on the hordes of excursionists drawn to Lundy to gaze at the expensive wreck of the HMS *Montagu*:

> Mr Heaven's residence stands near by the landing-place, and the venerable clergyman has long been a prominent figure, walking down to the beach occasionally, to gaze upon the people of the outer world, or to entrust some trustworthy-looking person with a letter to be posted; for in the official course it is only a weekly mail-service from Instow. The modern church of St.Helena, built at a cost of £6,500, was completed in 1897 and is capable of holding the entire population of Lundy, eight times over. Does any one expect active colonisation?

What turned out to be a couple of false alarms regarding the failure to sell the island in the early-1900s should be briefly mentioned – had the Heaven family actually sold then, the pattern of island transportation might have changed considerably. It was reported in August 1906 that a 'Continental Baron' was planning to purchase Lundy for £30,000 – and with it, he hoped, the rights to recover what remained of the HMS *Montagu* – to become an offshore Monte Carlo-style casino location, and what was later termed by the Revd

Heaven as a 'gambling hell' when he realised what was intended and rejected the offer. A few months later, in December 1906, another *Hartland Chronicle* report described an offer from the Revd Arthur Wellesley Batson to purchase the island for £30,000 – his plans were not disclosed. Either way, life on Lundy continued much as it had always done.

More pertinent to this account of the Lundy mailboats and how they got their cargoes ashore at various locations on a pierless and often windswept island, an article in the January 1911 edition of the *Hartland Chronicle* featuring Captain Dark and his experiences with *Gannet* shed light on the condition of the approaches to Pilots Quay, on the west side of the island. Rock-slides had made this alternative to the landing-beach difficult. In addition, Captain Dark recalled that a landslide some twenty years before had carried away the access to the point on the south end of the island known as Benjamin's Chair, alternatively known as The Rattles, or Rattles Landing Place. The significance of this account was that the difficulties of landing at Lundy had now become serious if conditions made the east side landing-beach untenable, and Captain Dark stated that there had been occasions of up to three months where an east-side landing had been impossible.

The Heaven family ownership of Lundy nevertheless continued with little potential for investment in any improved amenities. Amongst the last documented references to *Gannet* on a Lundy crossing was when she had given up her mailboat role. This was the sad occasion when, on 1 March 1916, the remains of the Revd Heaven – who had died at Torrington in the February of that year – were taken to Lundy from Instow for interment the next day. A final mention of *Gannet* – described as 'the old mailboat' – comes from an occasion documented in June 1918 when the Bishop of Exeter and a party which included the Rector and the Mayor of Bideford and others from Clovelly Court visited the church of St Helena on Lundy. (It should be made clear at this point that Walter Heaven, who had taken over the running of Lundy after his uncle from 1911, had no money with which to sustain a regular boat service contract with Dark, and so it must be assumed that this was a special charter of *Gannet* for the occasion.)

The end of Heaven family ownership was now in sight, with the Great War underway. However, to describe the packet story chronologically we must go back a few years, to the point where the mailboat role of *Gannet* was finally usurped by the steamer *Devonia*, under surprising circumstances.

The GANNET beached alongside Instow Quay. Some maintenance work appears to be taking place on a fore-sail.
DIANA KEAST COLLECTION

CHAPTER THREE

THE *DEVONIA* INTERLUDE

The last local steam packet service came into being in 1894 when the Bideford & Bristol Steamship Company Ltd. was floated at Bideford under the guiding influence of Edward J. Tattershill, the grocer . . . the Devonia, as their ship was called . . . was always remarkably well-kept and this, combined with the soundness of her design, led to a long and regular service. Her seaworthiness was remarkable . . .
GRAHAME FARR, *TRANSACTIONS OF THE DEVONSHIRE ASSOCIATION*, 1949.

In 1911, Captain Dark had decided to motorise his sailing-vessel *Gannet* to offer a more reliable service, and on seeking greater remuneration to cover his outlay was rebuffed by the Post Office, who had decided to put to competitive tender the Lundy mail contract. *Gannet* had been in service for over thirty years by then, and it seems remarkable that a vessel of that age should have been considered an appropriate beneficiary of the substantial investment needed to install the two-cylinder Fairbanks 7 b.h.p. single-screw engine, which by dint of the space consumed on board reduced her tonnage from 19 to 13

GRT. Captain Dark reckoned that he had spent at least £150 on the installation of the new machinery, and Post Office Records archive documents reveal that he sought payment of £112 p.a. for carrying the mails by his upgraded vessel. This was evidently thought – initially – by local Post Office officials to be quite reasonable, as it would give a more reliable service for the mails.

His 'notice to quit' was effective from 30 September 1911 and he clearly expected the new contract to be forthcoming, without expecting to be undercut. However, other boatmen in the vicinity thought they could

Low tide at Bideford Quay as the steam coaster DEVONIA, *owned by the Bideford and Bristol Steamship Co. Ltd., lies alongside between her weekly coasting voyages between the Torridge port and Bristol during the period 1894 to 1940. The shipping company offices, which offered 'Regular Steam Communication Between Bideford And Bristol', were nearby, at 9 North Road, Bideford, and the registered telegraphic address was* DEVONIA, BIDEFORD
MEDINA GALLERY, BIDEFORD

SHIPPING ON THE QUAY, BIDEFORD

offer more competitive rates to secure the seemingly desirable Post Office Lundy mails contract, and Captain Hocking of Appledore, in a letter dated 23 August 1911 offered the services of his boat, *Morning Star*, at £57 p.a. for the same level of weekly service, departing Instow on Thursdays at 06.00 and returning at 11.00 from Lundy. Given the opportunity to rethink, Captain Dark re-tendered on 29 August at £150 p.a., and again on 30 August at the rate of £125 p.a. The Post Office, having gone this far down the road of competitive tendering, now had no choice but to award the postal contract to Captain Hocking. Higher authorities had also been invoked by this stage. Performance clauses had probably not been heard of then, and no reference to reliability appears to have featured in the volley of correspondence on record. Captain Dark continued to operate for the Heaven family interests, but now without the Post Office income to supplement the supply-boat payments.

Captain Hocking soon found that he could not perform his new obligations effectively, and requested that his contract to carry the mails be terminated, as he had found that for his payment of little more than £1 per trip the provision of a weekly service to Lundy by his smack *Morning Star* was too time consuming, and thus not profitable. He gave notice to quit to the Post Office, in a handwritten letter dated 12 March 1912. We have already heard of the Bideford & Bristol Steamship Co. Ltd. who, since 1894, had been running their steamship *Devonia* on Bristol Channel packet duties, and the local company management were clearly already aware of Hocking's problem, as their Secretary, John Tucker, wrote to the Postmaster at Barnstaple on 7 March 1912 offering to convey the mails for the sum of £75 per annum. It is easy to infer that the Post Office only realised when it was too late that by terminating their arrangement with Captain Dark and his newly-improved *Gannet* they had created a problem for themselves on costs. Mr Tucker had already written to the Post Office as early as the previous November to remind them that the services of the Bideford & Bristol Steamship

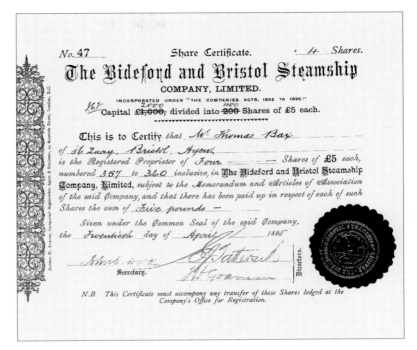

Co. Ltd. would be available 'should the opportunity arise'.

Devonia was at that time routinely engaged in a weekly run for her owners between Bideford and Bristol, carrying general merchandise. It was therefore a fairly straightforward matter for her schedule to be adjusted to incorporate Lundy calls, and the offer made was that *Devonia* would collect the mails at Instow whilst outward bound from Bideford, provided that they could be handed over to a Post Office official on the beach at Lundy. In the reverse direction, the same stipulation applied at Lundy when *Devonia* called on the return voyage from Bristol to Bideford. A proviso was made that if through stress of weather it was not possible to hand over the outward mails from the island at Instow Post Office, then they would be transferred at Ilfracombe. Finally, Mr Tucker requested that any telegrams transmitted in connection with the service should be free of charge.

The offer was accepted, and a formal contract drawn up, with effect from 18 March 1912. The contract contained various details of how the new service would work, and Mondays were set down as the day on which the mails would be both taken to and collected

Share certificate for the Bideford and Bristol Steamship Co. Ltd.
AUTHOR'S COLLECTION.

DEVONIA at Bideford. She has a trim, purposeful look.
IAN ARNOLD COLLECTION

from Lundy. The running of *Devonia* enabled an improvement in postal services to Lundy to be provided, as it was possible for *Devonia* to convey mail from Bristol to Lundy on her return voyage to Bideford on Wednesdays. By June 1912, a Post Office Circular Instruction had been issued which advised all Sorting Offices that if outward mail destined to Lundy missed the primary Monday sailing from Instow, then it could be directed instead to Bristol, provided that this was no later than by the Tuesday night mail train service, for onwards transmission to *Devonia's* Bristol berth at Narrow Quay. As a minor detail the postal address of Lundy was now formally defined as

Lundy Island, Devon rather than Lundy Island, Instow, Devon as previously.

This seemed a very practical new arrangement, albeit somewhat unpalatable to Captain Dark who still continued to service Lundy as required by the owners, believed then to be fortnightly, but without the guaranteed postal contract income. The coaster *Devonia* was no stranger to Lundy anyway, and photographs exist of her landing cattle there whilst beached between tides. The *Hartland Chronicle*, on Thursday 21 March 1912 duly recorded the first official *Devonia* Lundy Packet sailing; ' . . . ss Devonia took out the mails on Thursday 14th, and brought the return mail on Saturday . . . '. This is an interesting piece of evidence as straightaway, in that first week of the new regime, the outward mail day for Lundy was not in accordance with the agreed contract, and the level of postal service enjoyed by the Heaven family on Lundy would be subject to other external factors – those of weather and cargo loading considerations – compared to the dedicated service offered by Captain Dark on his purely local service.

Referring to the improved twice-weekly service a little later in the year the *Ilfracombe Gazette*, on Friday 24 May 1912, adopted what might be seen as a slightly patronising attitude to the communications deficiencies that islanders had had to endure when the mails were carried by the sailing skiff *Gannet*:

> . . . commencing this week Lundy Island will have the privilege of having two deliveries of the postbag a week instead of one. By this means the islanders will be able to keep themselves informed of events passing on the mainland, about which many have surprisingly little knowledge. One Lundy resident, who has not been off the island for a very long time, told a press representative that he had never seen a motor car.

The contrast in character with her mailboat predecessor *Gannet* was extreme, and *Devonia* was of course Bideford rather than Barnstaple registered. The Custom House Register entry, dated from her first registration on 19 February 1894 when new, read as follows:

No.	95919
Port	Bideford
Port no.	4/1894
Built	British-built
Type	Screw, steamship
Where built	Irvine, Gilmour & Co., 1894
Description	One deck, two masts, schooner-rigged, elliptic-stern
Tonnage	99.65 gross registered tons
Build	Clencher, iron transverse framework
Length	85 ft.
Breadth	18 ft.
Depth	7 ft 6 ins. (in hold)
Machinery	Compound, Direct-Acting, inverted Muir & Houston, two cylinders 12 ins. & 24 ins., 18 ins. stroke, 20 NHP, 9.5 knots
Ownership	Bideford & Bristol Steamship Company Ltd. 29 Bridgeland Street, Bideford, Devon

Lundy's second mailboat from 1912 (discounting the brief periods of service given fleetingly by *Queen of the Bay* and *Morning Star*) was, on the face of it, a logical progression from the first in 1878. However, the Great War soon intervened and although it is not wholly clear how postal services to the island were sustained during hostilities, Post Office archive documents indicate that the mail run carried out by *Devonia* ceased in 1916, and that mail was subsequently carried by Naval vessels. The postmaster at Barnstaple, in a later memo,

Invoice of the Bideford and Bristol Steamship Co. Ltd.
AUTHOR'S COLLECTION.

DEVONIA is seen here steaming through Bristol's City Docks, doubtless returning home to Bideford. For a brief period from 1911, she ran via Lundy to carry the mails, and thus connected Lundy with the Post Office at Bristol as well as at Instow.
GRAHAME FARR COLLECTION, COURTESY NIGEL COOMBES

pointed out that whilst the service offered by *Devonia* had been 'theoretically good' it had in practice been 'highly unsatisfactory', from which one deduces that the Lundy mails had not necessarily always had top priority in the affairs of the Bideford & Bristol Steamship Co. Ltd. This would, of course, have been exacerbated by the effects of the extreme Bristol Channel tides as well as the weather.

The final part of this chapter is to mention that Lundy changed hands in 1918 when the last member of the Heaven family sold, to Augustus Langham Christie of Tapeley Park, near Instow. In the period that elapsed before Christie purchased his own island vessel, the Bideford and Bristol Steamship Co. Ltd. made another offer to the Post Office, to carry the mails and all other traffic for what then seemed an exorbitant £25 per trip! Not surprisingly this offer was rejected, as it was clear that under new ownership Lundy might move towards greater self-sufficiency if an adequate boat were dedicated to island requirements. *Devonia* thus moved out of the mailboat succession, and gave way to *Lerina*,

although she still featured in the area in the general coasting trade until mined and lost in 1940. She had acquired a reputation for being a stout, well-run vessel, and one which rendered assistance to others on a number of occasions. Captain George Beer had command of her for over 40 years, most of the life of the vessel, and when he died at the end of 1946 at the age of 81, an obituary article published in the *Bideford Gazette* described some of these occasions. During the Great War, when running the mails to Lundy, Captain Beer had sighted the periscope of an enemy submarine near the island, and although *Devonia* survived unscathed, a Dominion Line vessel was torpedoed but saved, and the submarine sunk by destroyers. On another occasion, in January 1914, the steamship *Collier* was wrecked in Rockham Bay, west of Ilfracombe, and the lifeboat was towed to the scene by *Devonia*, and successfully rescued the crew of seven from the ship's boat. Described as being very much attached to his ship, Captain Beer retired in 1939.

Little can be traced nowadays of the coasting role that *Devonia* fulfilled over her life of almost half a century, but Grahame Farr, in a short paper to the Devonshire Association in June 1949, told the story of 'The Torridge, Devonia and other Bideford-Bristol steamers' which described various very early Bristol Channel steamers which plied that route with varying degrees of success in the nineteenth century. A step forward had been taken when the Bideford & Bristol Steamship Co. Ltd. was formed in 1894 in order to operate *Devonia*, on a co-operative basis by a number of traders without the motive of profit. He described the vessel, purpose-built for a Bristol Channel coasting role, and mentioned Lundy duties:

The Devonia . . . had a compound two-cylinder engine situated aft, and a small quarter-deck and forecastle deck. She was always remarkably well kept and this, combined with the soundness of her design, led to a long and regular service. Her seaworthiness was remarkable, for on many occasions she was active when other vessels were wrecked, and herself helped in the work of rescue . . . The main service of the Devonia was between Bideford and Bristol, but the coming of the motor-lorry and the greater use of the railway during the first world war caused this trade to diminish. She then went into the general coasting trade and, for a period, also ran mails and passengers to Lundy. At the end of the war her ownership was changed to the Devonia Steamship Company Limited, until in 1938 she was purchased by A. J. Smith Ltd. of Bristol. While in their coasting service she was mined in the Bristol Channel on 28th October, 1940 with the loss of all but one of her crew.

And so the story moves on, after the sailing boat *Gannet* and the steam coaster *Devonia* to the third Lundy Packet, of a very different character but which represented a reversion to a dedicated island link with the mainland for the new owner of Lundy, rather than perpetuating a dependency on more widely-spread interests.

DEVONIA beached at Lundy to load cattle, on a Lundy commercial postcard dated 1919. This card was loaned to the author by Don Mayes, who married Ava Zoref on Lundy in 1953, and to whom the card had been sent as a Christmas greeting in 1968 by Felix Gade, himself still then the resident Agent on Lundy. Mrs and Mr. Gade were known respectively as Cheerful and Gi, and the message on the card apologised for its lateness, as LUNDY GANNET had been delayed in taking the Christmas mail out to Lundy that year, not arriving until Christmas Eve.
DON MAYES COLLECTION

S.S. 'DEVONIA' LOADING CATTLE AT LUNDY, CIRCA 1919

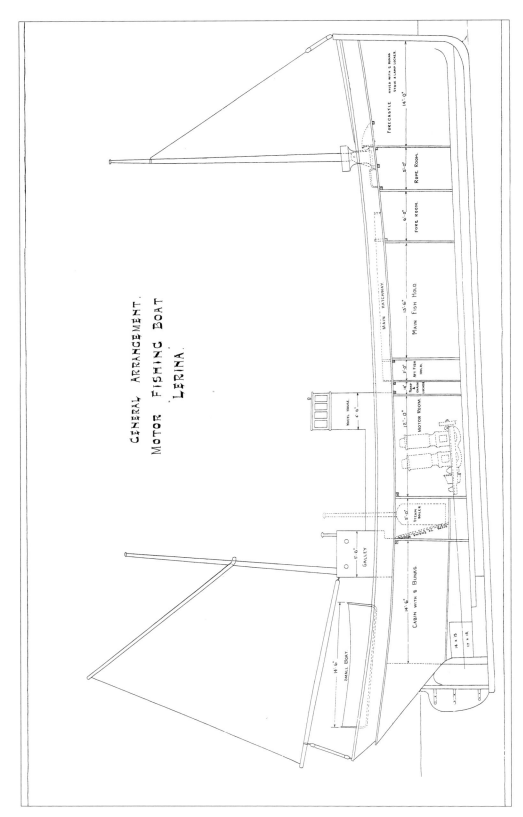

GENERAL ARRANGEMENT.
MOTOR FISHING BOAT
"LERINA".

General Arrangement drawing of LERINA *in her original as-built condition.*
NATIONAL MARITIME MUSEUM

CHAPTER FOUR
THE LONG REIGN
OF *LERINA*

I got to know the skipper of the Lerina, Frederick W. Dark, an outstanding example of a race of men who, regrettably, are dying out. He spent his life at sea in very small ships having been mate in his father's cutter, the Gannet, which had tended on Lundy and had carried the mails for many years prior to the purchase of the Lerina, a former motor drifter.
FELIX GADE, *MY LIFE ON LUNDY*

These words were written in 1973 by Felix Gade, the long-serving Resident Agent on Lundy during most of the period 1926 to 1970, and neatly sum up the Dark family connection with the mailboats during the nineteenth and twentieth centuries as well as through changes of ownership of Lundy.

The now motorised *Gannet* had ceased sailing regularly between Instow and Lundy. Frederick Dark had succeeded his father as Captain on the latter's retirement in 1915 and the ownership of the vessel was re-registered in February of that year from father to son. It is thought that occasional runs to Lundy were still provided, but with each voyage on a one-off basis as the Heaven family finances did not then permit the expense of a contracted service. The steam coaster *Devonia* had commenced the mail contract in 1912, but Post Office records state that around 1916 this involvement ceased. The naval trawler *Robert Davidson* had assumed the role of mailboat, more by default than by design under wartime conditions. This link was latterly with Milford Haven, in South Wales.

The purchase of Lundy by Augustus Langham Christie in 1918 prompted the acquisition of an almost new vessel to serve the transport needs of the island. Christie was the son of William Langham Christie of Glyndebourne and, on his father's death in 1913, had inherited a very substantial 10,000 acre estate with grounds at Glyndebourne, as well as extensive properties in Devon which included Tapeley Park near Instow and much of Braunton Burrows. The Christie family had long owned the shore at Instow, and had

derived income from ferry rights between that town, Braunton and Appledore across the River Torridge through charging ferrymen for the use of Instow Quay, which dated from the seventeenth century. It was said that Christie had a desire to own all that he could see from his home at Tapeley Park, which provided a reason for his purchase of Lundy although little evidence remains of precisely what he intended to do with the property as he did not take up permanent residence on the island, being content to initially retain the services as Manager of a Mr Dennis until 1920, and then to appoint a Mr C. H. May as lessee for the rest of his period of ownership. Christie is believed to have rarely visited Lundy but he did take action to restore buildings on the island which had lapsed into a neglected state.

The former Lowestoft motor drifter *Lerina* thus enters the Lundy Packet succession as representing the new order after the Great War. Fred Dark accepted the captaincy of this vessel from the time of its acquisition by Lundy's new owner, and was destined to stay with his boat through the next change of ownership of Lundy in 1925, providing great local knowledge and continuity. The Barnstaple Shipping Register records that *Gannet* was sold in November 1923 to a Mr Edward Henry Read of The Old Custom House, Pill, Somerset. In 1938 Fred Darks's daughter V. E. Dark stated that the vessel then lay at Southampton, and had not been broken up. Fred Dark's father, William Dark, died in February 1926.

The vessel chosen on behalf of Christie was the almost new *Lerina*, built in 1917 by Colby Bros at Oulton Broad, Lowestoft and originally in the ownership of Lowestoft Steam Herring Drifters Ltd. Her career there was short, and it is of interest that of the many hundreds of fishing vessels built at Lowestoft by the company (known by 1919 as John Chambers Limited, Shipbuilders & Engineers) virtually all were either sailing or steam-vessels apart from three which were motor-vessels, of which two were British-registered and one Swedish. Motor propulsion was then innovative. An attractive vessel, with plentiful sheer, the details of the dimensions and machinery of *Lerina* recorded in the Barnstaple Custom House Register of Shipping under Christie's outright ownership on 15 August 1919 were as follows:

No.   139979
Port   Barnstaple
Port no.   2/1919 (prev. 32 in 1917 at Lowestoft)
Built   British-built
Type   Motor, Single-Screw
Where built   Colby Bros, Oulton Broad, 1917

This view of LERINA is believed to be of her 'maiden' Lundy voyage post-refit, duly dressed and looking pristine, on Saturday 12 August 1922. She had been in service to Lundy for just under three years by this time, and represented the hopes and aspirations of the new owner Augustus Langham Christie and his lessee C.H.May for development of the island for tourism, aided by the opening up of the Manor Farm Hotel for those wishing to stay for longer than just a day-trip.
TOM BAKER COLLECTION

Description	One deck, two masts, dandy-rigged, semi-elliptical-stern
Tonnage	30.63 gross registered tons (subsequently 46.06 after 1922 refit)
Build	Carvel, wood framework motor fishing vessel, one bulkhead (two), no ballast tanks
Length	78.6 ft.
Breadth	18.7 ft.
Depth	8 ft 6 ins. (in hold), length of engine-room 12.5 ft.
Machinery	Hot Bulb Crude Oil Motor, foreign (Bolinder, Stockholm), two cylinders 12 $\frac{63}{64}$th ins. each diameter, 13 $\frac{3}{8}$ ins stroke, 80 BHP, about 8 knots

She did not enter Lundy service straightaway, and according to Post Office records the circumstances surrounding the expedient delivery of the mails during the war and in the immediate postwar years were problematic. The naval trawler *Robert Davidson*

Lundy Royal Mail Motor Yacht "Lerina".

had been carrying the mails from Ilfracombe since 1916, but from 22 January 1919 came under the jurisdiction of the Naval Commanding Officer at Milford Haven and ran from there to Lundy. As well as catering for the needs of the residents on Lundy the naval trawler also serviced the island Coastguard requirements, including the transport of personnel, fuel and supplies as well as carrying naval mail. *Lerina* was stated to be still undergoing repairs in April 1920, but the Royal Navy clearly wanted to withdraw from their commitment after hostilities had ceased. In a letter dated 8 April 1920 from the Commanding Officer of the Milford Haven Naval Base to the Milford Haven Postmaster it was stated that the *Robert Davidson* would be paid off on 20 April 1920, and after that date would cease carrying the mails to Lundy Island.

This left the Post Office with an immediate problem. Christie obviously saw that a solution lay in him offering to undertake the mail carrier duties by his *Lerina*, and proposed to do so for a fee of £100 p.a. The Postmaster felt that this amount was high relative to the volume of mail involved, but after receiving a quote from the Bideford & Bristol Steamship Company Ltd. to carry out the mail run on new terms of £25 per trip, clearly had little choice but to accept Christie's terms. A new contract was drawn up, which looked substantially like the one that had been in place between the Post Office and the Bideford & Bristol Steamship Company from 1912 onwards, but with the crucial difference that three parties were now involved, namely the Post Office and the Admiralty jointly, and Augustus Langham Christie. Christie, and his agents, had clearly bargained hard as the amount documented in the Contract was a payment of £208 p.a., that is, £104 p.a. from each of the two joint parties – the Post Office and the Admiralty. The designated mail day was now Friday, and the Contract was dated to take effect from 31 December 1920.

It is clear that *Lerina* actually commenced her new duties well before the date formally agreed in the new contract and an early example of her going to the rescue of a vessel

in distress was recorded in the *Hartland Chronicle* in June 1920 when she had assisted the schooner *Dundarg*, bound from Runcorn to Fowey, whose anchor had dragged near Lundy. *Lerina* had taken the mails to the island, saw distress signals from the schooner, and promptly went to her assistance, towing her to a safe anchorage off the island, where it

A cheerful looking group on board LERINA *probably sometime during the period 1920-5, left to right Captain Fred Dark, the secretary to C.H.May, and C.H.May (lessee) himself.*
MYRTLE TERNSTROM COLLECTION

A shot doubtless from the same voyage; Jack Branch, Engineer, is on the right
MYRTLE TERNSTROM COLLECTION

INSTOW QUAY FROM MARINE HOTEL. 37

A commercial postcard showing LERINA at anchor in the River Torridge off Instow Quay. TOM BAKER COLLECTION

was stated that around 200 other vessels were weather-bound. In the meantime the Lundy Coastguard had communicated with the mainland, and the Clovelly lifeboat put off to assist *Dundarg*. The lifeboat crew then stopped on board *Lerina* for the night and the lifeboat was towed back to Clovelly by *Lerina* the following day.

Whilst *Lerina* was based at the Dark family home-port of Instow, as *Gannet* had been before her, and mailboat sailings ran from there in accordance with the Post Office contract, she would handle passengers from Appledore as well, and carried her own fourteen-foot pulling-boat to tender at either side of the River Torridge, the two ports being approximately opposite one another. The proximity of Instow railway station to Instow Quay was convenient for travellers to Lundy as through trains from London Waterloo to the West Country ran *via* Exeter and Barnstaple to Ilfracombe, Bideford and beyond and called at Instow on the attractive single track railway line which skirted the Taw and Torridge estuaries. The substantial Marine Hotel at Instow also acted as a convenient point of

embarkation or disembarkation for the intrepid Lundy mailboat traveller, also being situated virtually adjacent to Instow Quay. Compared with the sparseness of a passage in an open sailing-boat like *Gannet* before her, the new, somewhat faster and larger *Lerina* must have indeed seemed a tremendous improvement, although concessions to creature comforts onboard were few.

Lerina was not initially intended to handle any significant numbers of Lundy excursion passengers and, as we have seen, before the Great War the Pockett steamers had provided the principal excursion link from Ilfracombe to Lundy since the 1860s. Ilfracombe grew rapidly in status as a resort in the closing years of the nineteenth century. From about 1911 onwards the P. & A. Campbell Ltd. steamers added Lundy to their range of regular excursion destinations from the up-Channel ports of Bristol and Cardiff and the various seaside piers that evolved in the Bristol Channel at resorts such as Weston-super-Mare, Clevedon, Minehead and Penarth. Whilst the offering by Pockett's elderly paddle-steamer *Brighton* was weekly, or occasionally twice-weekly, Swansea and Mumbles to Lundy *via* Ilfracombe excursion sailings, the White Funnel Fleet might typically run once a week to Lundy, and would sometimes be routed *via* Clovelly. In the heyday of the White Funnel Fleet in the period around 1912-14 ten vessels ran in the Bristol Channel, and often one might see four or even five of these beautiful ships tied up during the afternoon at Ilfracombe Harbour, having run down-channel during the morning to give their day-tripper passengers a few hours ashore in that most attractive Devon port. After the war their fleet strength was seriously depleted, and in 1919 the few vessels they had available were concentrated on the upper Bristol Channel 'ferry' duties between Cardiff and Newport and Bristol, Weston and Clevedon with very few trips all the way down to Ilfracombe, and none proceeding out to Lundy.

Pockett's passenger excursion sailings did not recommence after the Great War, and the White Funnel Fleet established a presence at Swansea in lieu of these. For the 1920 season the strengthened fleet of Bristol Channel vessels enabled Lundy excursions to recommence, but at this stage no attempt was made by the P. & A. Campbell Ltd. to run excursions from the Torridge estuary and the decision was taken by Mr C. H. May that *Lerina* would be refitted to cater for a greater number of passengers. Mr May, the Lundy lessee, had ambitions to increase trade to the island and boost visitor numbers at the recently-opened Manor Farm Hotel. Scrutiny of surviving Christie accounts for the period throw an interesting light on this decision, inasmuch as expenditure on running *Lerina* greatly exceeded income; in 1920 the former amounted to just under £2,000 whilst income only totalled around half of that sum. Within this poor operating ratio was contained, exceptionally, the sum of £150 received as salvage in respect of assistance rendered by *Lerina* to the distressed schooner *Dundarg*; passenger ticket receipts totalled only £60, much of the income balance deriving from the proceeds of fish and lobster catches.

Shortly before the inaugural sailing of the improved *Lerina*, an event took place on

Simply entitled 'Landing stores at Lundy', this postcard conveyed a tranquil image, probably of the 1920/30s era. Diana Keast remembered selling copies of it in The Store. The building a little way up the road (right) was known as 'Sea View', and used for storage of lobster-pots and the like. Also visible is the cave, where dinghies could be stored.
ALAN KITTRIDGE
COLLECTION

6304. Landing Stores, Lundy.

This occasion on board LERINA *was the return of Walter Heaven's ashes to Lundy in 1930, left to right Jack Branch (Engineer), Captain Fred Dark, Revd Muller, and Tommy Hornabrook. The Revd Muller of Appledore was a frequent visitor to Lundy through until the 1950s, often on the White Funnel Fleet steamers where he was well known to Officers and crew.*
MYRTLE TERNSTROM
COLLECTION

Lundy which attracted considerable attention and was to boost awareness of the charms of the island to visitors. As the weekly newspaper *The Ilfracombe Chronicle & North Devon News* put it, Wednesday 9 August 1922 was '. . . a red-letter day in the annals of Lundy Island, the occasion being the formal institution and induction of the Revd Henry Hezekiah Lane – the first Rector the island has had for 567 years.' Since the death of the Revd H. G. Heaven, the Revd Swatridge had been appointed, but he left Lundy in 1916. Responsibility for the spiritual oversight of the island had then been vested in Mr F. W. Allday, the postmaster of Lundy who as a Lay Reader conducted services at the Church of St Helena. The event prompted a large party to travel to the island from the 'magnificient steamboat Devonia' – the former Red Funnel Line paddle-steamer which had become a White Funnel Fleet member in 1912. In his address to the congregation, the Bishop of Crediton, Dr Trefusis, explained that the parish boundary of Lundy stretched for three miles around the island, and alluded to the huge number of vessels which passed by Lundy every year – about a million, he understood

(*sic*) – adding that the ministry of the Revd H. H. Lane would include providing spiritual care for the men in those ships. Sadly for Lundy and the new incumbent, the Revd Lane, this arrangement was not to last very long, as his resignation took effect in June 1924, after which time Lundy was looked after by the Vicar of Appledore.

Early in 1922 *Lerina* had undergone alterations at the Appledore yard of P. K. Harris to increase her passenger accommodation to forty. This was achieved by the addition of two new deckhouses, one each fore and aft of the wheelhouse, and a pair of lifeboats. Her tonnage increased correspondingly. A ladder descended to the engine compartment forward, and the crew accommodation aft. Original General Arrangement drawings show that eight bunks were provided, but Mr Gade later stated that accommodation for four crew was provided, and that *Lerina* normally ran with a crew of three; the master Fred Dark, the mate Jack Branch and the engineer Abbott. One week after the rector's induction, the *The Ilfracombe Chronicle & North Devon News* reported that the improvements made to the refitted *Lerina* were 'through the initiative of the lessee C. Herbert May', and noted that ornithologists visiting Lundy would be particularly keen to avail themselves of the enhanced mailboat facilities in view of the significance of the island being the breeding place of many rare birds.

What was described as the vessel's 'Official Trial Trip' took place on Saturday 12 August 1922 and the *The Ilfracombe Chronicle & North Devon News* succinctly described what happened, and what a stay on Lundy had to offer:

The vessel's seaworthiness was fully demonstrated on the official trial trip from Bideford and Instow on Saturday, undertaken in rather unkind weather for August, when some 30 guests accepted the owner's invitation to visit Lundy. Despite the weather, the visitors found much to interest them on the island after luncheon at the Manor House Hotel, and those whose first visit it was were particularly delighted with the beautiful church of St Helena, the gift to the Exeter Diocese of the late Revd H. G. Heaven, a former owner of Lundy. The island covers a total area of 1,047 acres, and on the farm Mr May has a considerable number of cattle and sheep, whilst corn of very good quality is grown. The luxuriance of the flowering shrubs in the delightful ornamental walks between the hotel and the villa is almost tropical, and attributable to the climate, which is far more equable than that of the mainland, long observation having proved it to be 7 degrees warmer in winter and 7 degrees cooler in summer. Situated in the great waterway to the South Wales and Bristol ports, there is always something of interest to be seen passing the island, whilst the abundance of good sport to be obtained by sea-fishermen is making Lundy increasingly popular each summer. The Manor House is a well-equipped hotel, enlarged some time since, and with provision for a large number of visitors.

The ideal means of reaching Lundy during the season is via Ilfracombe, and from thence by one of Messrs P. & A. Campbell's magnificent and popular steamboats, which make occasional visits to the island during the season.

Although *Lerina* had been refitted to cater for more passengers, there was recognition that the best interests of island tourism were served by P. & A. Campbell Ltd.'s sailings, seen as complementary to rather than in competition with her trips. Comparative fare levels were of note, a day-trip by *Lerina* to Lundy cost seven shillings and sixpence from either Bideford, Barnstaple or Instow, whilst a P. & A. Campbell Ltd. sailing all the way from Cardiff to Lundy was offered at nine shillings and sixpence, albeit usually giving a rather shorter stay ashore. The White Funnel Fleet steamers occasionally offered Round Lundy non-landing cruises, at a fare of nine shillings from Cardiff.

The schedules offered by the Lundy mailboat at this time make fascinating reading, and *Lerina* made a number of sailings from Barnstaple Quay. Bideford and Appledore departures also featured prominently in her schedules, the former being about twenty minutes sailing time up the River Torridge beyond Instow and Appledore. A sailing bill, carried in the *North Devon Journal* for the week ending Sunday 27 August 1922 for the 'Royal Mail Motor Yacht Lerina', listed departures from Barnstaple to Lundy on Thursday 24, Friday 25 and Sunday 27 August, which called at Instow 30 minutes later. The departure on Saturday 26 was from Bideford, after which the Instow call took place 20 minutes later. The bill also referred to an Afternoon Service at St Helena's Church on Lundy on Sunday 27 given by the Revd H. H. Lane, Rector of Lundy. The mails at this time were specifically advertised as being carried on the Friday sailings. Tides wholly dictated what was possible as sailing times in the Rivers Taw and Torridge, and some Lundy trips commenced at Instow. For example during the following week that on Wednesday 30 August 1922, also advertised a connecting departure from Appledore that would have necessitated the use of another local launch from the ferry steps on Appledore Quay.

The sailing bill for *Lerina* for the week ending Sunday 17 September 1922 was an interesting one and advertised a number of trips other than just routine Lundy runs. Thus, *Lerina* was programmed to make day trips to Lundy on Monday, Tuesday,

LERINA ticket 1922-3
TOM BAKER COLLECTION

15.00 for the sum of 6d. Just as nowadays, the total dependency on tides dictated a certain expediency in scheduling, and *Lerina* offered a short Bar Trip on the Saturday from Appledore and Instow at 13.30. The climax for Captain Dark of this busy week of sailings for *Lerina* was a Special Long Day Trip advertised on the Sunday from Clovelly to Lundy, leaving Clovelly at 09.30 and not returning from Lundy until 18.00.

In 1923 the sailings offered by *Lerina* followed a similar pattern to that established the previous year and typically an advertisement in the *Bideford Gazette* newspaper would list two weeks worth of departures to Lundy in the summer period. On days with suitable tides sailings would normally be offered from Bideford with calls *en route* at Instow and Appledore, or from Barnstaple. The River Taw did not then present such an obstacle to navigation as now, and a spring tide period might see three successive days of Barnstaple departures for Lundy. Friday remained the mail-day, and on other days when tides were less suitable for River Torridge sailings, Clovelly to Lundy trips were occasionally on offer. Sailings were, of course, subject to the customary caveat 'wind, weather and other circumstances permitting' but the general feeling was that *Lerina* was a reliable vessel, and that whatever the conditions prevailing on arrival at Lundy Captain Dark would always find somewhere to get the mailbag, at least, ashore.

Henry Wentworth Jukes, a member of the Lundy Coastguard establishment writing in 1920, described the difficulties that *Gannet* had when conditions made the landing beach untenable, and noted that improvements were made by Christie as a matter of some priority. Large quantities of rock at the entrance to the Cove were blasted away to make it easier and safer for a vessel to approach and beach itself there, rather than be wholly reliant on the main landing beach. A jetty was constructed on top of a ledge of rocks, which ran from the foreshore, which it was intended would run right to low water mark and provide the best landing place on the island. (The new pier of 1999 lies adjacent.) Felix Gade recorded the

Wednesday and Friday, the first three being from Bideford, Appledore and Instow and the Friday one – 'Carrying the Royal Mails', as passengers again were proudly reminded – not serving Bideford. The bill stated that:

N.B. For passengers from Westward Ho! and District arrangements have been made to facilitate embarking and disembarking at Appledore. Enquire OATWAY, Grand Hotel, Appledore.

However, on Thursday 14 September *Lerina* was advertised to run a day-trip at 11.15 from Appledore and Instow to Clovelly, with a coast cruise being offered from Clovelly at wide variety of landing-places occasionally resorted to by Captain Fred Dark when weather conditions required a degree of improvisation; aside from those already mentioned at Pilots Quay accessible to the unpowered *Gannet* and Montagu Steps (put there by Christie in 1920-1), use was made by *Lerina* in skilled hands of Smugglers Path (that is, the path from Rattles), and Hell's Gate. Further afield, although on the east coast and not necessarily a practical alternative in easterlies, Brazen Ward and Gannet's Bay occasionally featured. A glance at the photograph of the rungs Christie had fitted to the rock at the Montagu Steps location will be quite enough to make the point about travellers to Lundy needing an intrepid spirit if they were determined to reach the island come what may!

Not long after all the excitement associated with her expanded role had died down, it is apparent that the passenger-carrying capacity of the island mailboat *Lerina* had to be reduced, as it was found that the two substantial lifeboats added had impaired her stability and manoeuvrability. In addition, Captain Dark had been required to employ a suitably-qualified extra master as he only held what was described as a 'fishing-ticket', and the expense of this was significant. Reference to

the changes, which reduced the scope of the excursions provided by *Lerina*, was made by the late Mr A. E. Blackwell in an evocative account entitled *Some Personal Notes on a Visit to Lundy, 1925*. Mr Blackwell had journeyed by train to Instow, spending the night at the Marine Hotel before taking passage on *Lerina*:

> . . . awakening to the gleaming sunshine of an August morning with 'Appledore in Devon' winking at us across the estuary, we arose to the full enjoyment of contemplation of a passage to the island in the Lerina. That sturdy little craft was lying on the Appledore side and had suffered no greater eclipse than a repainting, since our last view of her, whereby she appeared with a black hull in lieu of the familiar white band as of yore. It transpired however that other changes had been at work which restricted her activities to the limit of carrying twelve passengers as a maximum, in infringement of which Board of Trade condition had landed Captain Fred Dark in a Police Court. Captain Dark was interviewed early and announced noon or shortly after as his sailing time . . . there was much talk by the time Lerina had tossed her way over the miles of choppy water, with Bull Point away to the starboard and Hartland away to port, and had brought up in her usual adroit style within easy reach of Lundy's ever-hospitable beach . . .

LERINA did not run for long with the two lifeboats in davits installed during her 1922 refit. The steps carried on her port-side are clearly visible in this view, which was used for a commercial postcard.
TOM BAKER COLLECTION

Beach scene at Lundy entitled 'Lundy mail coming ashore in small boat' from the collection of the late A.E.Blackwell of Instow
COURTESY MYRTLE TERNSTROM

The next event of moment in the history of *Lerina* occurred as a result of the purchase of Lundy Island by a wealthy city financier, Martin Coles Harman. Born in 1888, he had since his childhood days harboured ambitions to own Lundy and when the Christie Estate put the island to auction with the agents Knight, Frank & Rutley he seized his opportunity. Rather than wait for the auction, he ascertained that a bid by private treaty of £12,000 had already been made, and promptly bid £16,000. His offer was accepted and he became the owner of Lundy Island, thus starting what was to become the final phase of private ownership of the Bristol Channel island. Christie had suffered from illness, described by one commentator as bouts of nervous instability. The Barnstaple Shipping Register had it on record that at the point of sale in February 1926 of *Lerina* to Martin Coles Harman to go with his newly-acquired island, ownership of all 64 shares of the vessel were in the name of his wife, Lady Rosamond Alicia Christie, his Receiver.

After a few months with an agent based in Weston-super-Mare Harman appointed Felix Gade (a friend from childhood days) as his resident Lundy Agent, who became the much respected senior island resident until the time of his retirement some forty or so years later. We are fortunate that his memoirs have been so diligently recorded, in the form of the very substantial autobiography *My Life on Lundy*, and numerous references to Lundy's maritime affairs are on record, especially regarding *Lerina*, as well as Mr Gade's great regard for her captain, Fred Dark, and the vicissitudes of dealing with all the problems that went with the comparative isolation of the island and its shipping needs. Of highly independent outlook, Harman did not reside full time on Lundy, but his determination to do things his way on his own private property soon became evident, and to this end Mr Gade was a faithful ally.

Having acquired the boat to go with the island, Harman rapidly discovered that the expenses of running her greatly outweighed

Stores coming ashore at Lundy, with LERINA *in the background.*
MYRTLE TERNSTROM
COLLECTION

the income received through the Post Office contract. Initially, the contract between Christie, the Post Office and the Admiralty was reassigned to Harman after the purchase of the island, and was effective from July 1926. Shortly after this formal transfer of interest, Mr J. G. Laithwaite, the Postal Surveyor at Exeter, wrote to Mr Harman stating that the Postmaster General had agreed to the proposition that the sailing day be changed from Fridays to Wednesdays, and that the Admiralty had also agreed. This arrangement lasted into 1927.

However, it was logical for Harman to seek to reduce expenses. The outcome of discussion with Post Office officials led to the termination of the agreement for the Post Office presence on Lundy. The island sub-post office thus lost its 'official' status but, in return

for Harman undertaking to ship mail to Lundy at no charge to the Post Office, on the days when it suited him and the island's needs rather than on a contractually prescribed day, he would offset postal costs by charging for letters that came to and went off the island and keeping that revenue. Mr Gade thus became the island postmaster as part of his duties as Agent, and distributed incoming post after affixing special stamps and charging the islanders accordingly. Here were the beginnings of the famous Lundy stamps, now so collectable.

It is worth recalling the background of the presence of the Post Office on Lundy, and to note that Harman was keen to rid his island of anything he regarded as bureaucratic interference with his affairs. During much of the nineteenth century no Post Office presence

BOTTOM LEFT
Passengers landing at Lundy.
MYRTLE TERNSTROM
COLLECTION

BELOW
Landing a pony at Lundy, with F. W. Gade standing in the prow of the boat.
MYRTLE TERNSTROM
COLLECTION

A splendid view of the 1930s crew of LERINA: left to right, front, Bob Helson, Alf Branch and Jack Branch with Capt. Fred Dark behind, in charismatic trilby. Bob Helson was not actually a crew-member but was usually resident on Lundy and involved in a wide variety of tasks, and remembered as a great character.
MYRTLE TERNSTROM
COLLECTION

had existed on Lundy and *Gannet* ran essentially to serve the needs of the island which included, almost incidentally, the carriage of the mails. No formal mail contract was necessary with Captain William Dark until the Post Office presence on the island commenced. Things changed when a marine communications cable was laid in 1893 from Croyde. Mr F. Allday, a Naval pensioner employed originally by Lloyds of London, was appointed as the first sub-postmaster in 1898. A radical change was now in prospect for the mail service, linked to the retirement of Mr Allday in 1926 and a brief period when he was succeeded first by a Mr Lang, and then by a Mr Mien who had been Head Gardener. By the end of 1927 Mr Mien left and the idea had

already begun to formulate in the mind of Harman that he could do without the presence of the Post Office on his island kingdom, in furtherance of the desire to exclude mainland authorities.

It is clear from Post Office archives that as early as January 1927 Martin Coles Harman had ideas of issuing his own stamps. His preliminary offer to the Post Office proposed that, in order that he could be free to run *Lerina* at times suitable to the needs of himself and the island, if the Post Office would take outgoing mail from Lundy for onwards distribution at no charge, he then would undertake to carry mail from the mainland to Lundy free of charge, and distribute it amongst the islanders. This proposal was rejected as it would have meant delivering mail from Lundy on the mainland with only a Lundy stamp. At that point he gave notice that he would stick to the terms of the 1926 Agreement only until 1 April 1927. As a *quid pro quo*, he proposed that he recoup some of his own costs by making a charge on outgoing mails through the issue of his own stamps. In Mr Gade's memoirs it is recorded that this arrangement was not entered into straightaway, although there was a period during which the mails were carried free until 1 November 1929. The decision to issue stamps was taken in the summer of 1929 and the first produced were a pink 'half-puffin' and a blue 'one-puffin'. In this manner commenced a new era of philatelic interest in Lundy, albeit unwittingly in that Harman later stated (to Stanard, in the definitive postal history of Lundy *The Lundy Locals*) that he had no idea that so much interest would accrue to something devised as a functional arrangement to suit his own ends and beliefs. Harman also attempted to introduce his own coinage to Lundy, but officialdom thought otherwise and he was prosecuted in 1930. It was at the Appeal afterwards that he uttered the famous remark 'I dismissed the GPO'.

As far as the Lundy Packets story goes, this was the key event after which the mails carried the distinctive additional stamps. Air services commenced in the 1930s and the carriage of the mails became more of an intermittent story for the ships as a certain amount of airmail now passed in addition to the regular carriage of mails by sea. Thus *Lerina* sailed on, under the day to day management of Felix Gade who had been designated formally in Barnstaple Registry Transactions as the Ships Husband from the time of his first association with Lundy as Agent. Although Harman was adjudged bankrupt in 1932 following the collapse of his financial interests, life on Lundy carried on reasonably normally, and Mr Gade was designated as the Managing Owner of *Lerina* in 1935 following a series of transactions which effectively allowed Lundy to avoid seizure by Harman's receiver at that troubled time.

In the 1930s the Lundy mailboat scene had settled into a regular pattern, and *Lerina* fulfilled her duties from her Instow base under Fred Dark's continued captaincy. The Manor Farm Hotel on Lundy was promoted in literature produced by Mr Gade which featured the slogan 'Nature's Unspoilt Isle' and a simple message was used to convey an image of unhurried character and a simple way of life for those that sought tranquillity.

The text of a brochure of the period nicely put this into context alongside earlier years:

. . . until recently Lundy was a no-man's land, visitors were unwanted and unprovided for, landing dues were prohibitive, and its shores were only reached by the uncertain favour of the mailboat. The Manor Farm Hotel now affords comfortable accommodation and from the products of the Island provides simple wholesome fare. Between June 1st and September 30th a regular passenger service is maintained from Ilfracombe by Messrs P. & A. Campbell's passenger steamers, and all the year round the motor mailboat Lerina takes not exceeding ten passengers one day a week from Instow, or can be specially chartered by parties (not exceeding ten) embarking from Instow, Clovelly, Bideford, Ilfracombe, Tenby or Swansea. The passage from mainland to Lundy Island occupies about two hours.

The brochure added that the mail day was now Wednesday, with last posting on Tuesday.

The humdrum existence of *Lerina* was occasionally enlivened by the odd unplanned event such as a breakdown when, on 14 March

The LERINA at Lundy with a launch ferrying passengers. Note the carefully-gathered driftwood in the foreground. When this accumulated to a decent load it would be carted up to the village as a valuable source of fuel.
MYRTLE TERNSTROM COLLECTION

1937, she found herself with loss of power in a strong north-east breeze with high seas, poor visibility and in bitter cold drifting down Channel past Hartland. By flying a piece of red cloth as a distress signal and setting her own two small sails, *Lerina* was able to keep herself off the land and was towed into the safe haven of Padstow by the then almost new Clovelly motor lifeboat *City of Nottingham*, rather than attempt the difficult tow back up Channel. There have, over the years, been numerous instances recorded of the Clovelly lifeboat giving assistance to vessels near Lundy.

Later that year, it was the turn of *Lerina* to give assistance to passengers stranded on Lundy by P. & A. Campbell Ltd's paddle-steamer *Britannia*, on Thursday 16 September 1937. After arrival at Lundy from Bristol, passengers had gone ashore but 19 were left behind after re-embarkation became too risky

and the master of the paddler decided that worsening weather conditions meant he had to leave without further delay. On the next day, Friday, another White Funnel Fleet paddler, *Cambria*, crossed to Lundy and although conditions on the landing beach were still very difficult, the stranded passengers were eventually re-embarked after the crew of *Lerina* helped the *Cambria's* crew with the boat transfer by rigging a line between the landing launch and the dinghy bringing people off the beach, and hauling the dinghy off the beach by force using the line. As with many other incidents affecting the White Funnel Fleet steamers over the years this one, when recorded in the supportive language of the local Ilfracombe newspaper, generated a very positive image of heroism triumphing over adversity, and the courage of Captain Dark was fulsomely acknowledged in what had been dangerous and difficult circumstances. Such a situation nowadays would be differently interpreted and safety practices questioned.

Another, happier, incident in 1937 rounds off this glimpse of what life was like for *Lerina* and her crew before the Second World War

One imagines in this view that LERINA is about to leave Lundy and get underway for the mainland. Evidence of her port of registry of Barnstaple is visible in this atmospheric view.
MYRTLE TERNSTROM
COLLECTION

A deck view of LERINA with Mrs Gade (wife of Lundy Agent Felix Gade) on board in the 1930s
DIANA KEAST COLLECTION

LUNDY

•

DAY TRIPS BY
Motor Vessel "LERINA"

(WEATHER AND OTHER CIRCUMSTANCES PERMITTING):

Thursday, 31st August 1939

Leaving APPLEDORE (Bidna Wharf) ... 8.15 a.m.
„ INSTOW QUAY ... ... 8.30 a.m.
Arriving back at Instow approximately 7.0 p.m.

Saturday, 2nd Sept.

Leaving APPLEDORE (Bidna Wharf) ... at 8.30 a.m.
„ INSTOW QUAY ... ... „ 8.45 a.m.
Arriving back at Instow approximately 7.30 p.m.

Tuesday, 5th Sept.

Leaving APPLEDORE (Bidna Wharf) ... at 10.0 a.m.
„ INSTOW QUAY ... ... „ 10.15 a.m.
Arriving back at Instow approximately 9.0 p.m.

Thursday, 14th Sept.

Leaving APPLEDORE (Bidna Wharf) ... at 8.0 a.m.
„ INSTOW QUAY ... ... „ 8.15 a.m.
Arriving back at Instow approximately 7.0 p.m.

Saturday, 16th Sept.

Leaving APPLEDORE (Bidna Wharf) ... at 8.30 a.m.
„ INSTOW QUAY ... ... „ 8.45 a.m.
Arriving back at Instow approximately 7.30 p.m.

Tuesday, 19th Sept.

Leaving APPLEDORE Bidna Wharf) ... at 10.30 a.m.
„ INSTOW QUAY ... ... „ 10.45 a.m.
Arriving back at Instow approximately 10.0 p.m.

―――――――――――――――――――

SPECIAL TRIPS CAN BE ARRANGED

―――――――――――――――――――

RETURN FARE 10/- (Payable at time of booking) including

embarking and disembarking at Instow and Lundy and landing fee at Lundy.

Accommodation being strictly limited passengers are advised to secure bookings, as far in advance as possible, from :—
Capt. F. Dark, 2, Elm Terrace, INSTOW, 'Phone INSTOW 21.
Robert Helson, 2, Silver Street, APPLEDORE.
Harper's Library, High Street, BIDEFORD, 'Phone BIDEFORD 173.
Lundy & Atlantic Coasts Air Lines, Ltd., North Devon Aerodrome, Heanton Court, BARNSTAPLE, 'Phone BRAUNTON 121. Or from
Alfred E. Blackwell, 1, Craigwell Villas, INSTOW, 'Phone, INSTOW 58.

―――――――――――――――――――

Excellent Accommodation at the MANOR FARM HOTEL
LUNCHEON 2/6 LOBSTER LUNCHEON 3/- TEA 1/3

―――――――――――――――――――

GAZETTE PRINTING SERVICE, GRENVILLE STREET, BIDEFORD.

intervened. The engineer, John Branch, made the news when it was reported that he was very nearly late for his wedding on account of unavoidable delays at Lundy. He was due to be married at St Marys Parish Church at Appledore at 2.30 p.m. on Thursday 23 September, but *Lerina* was unavoidably detained at Lundy until 11.30 that morning. What would normally have been a three hour passage for the twenty mile voyage was that day reduced to 2 hrs 35 minutes, despite a heavy ground sea and head winds, but Mr Branch evidently just made it to the church on time by being collected by Captain Victor Lesslie (the senior Trinity pilot at Appledore) at W. J. Lamey's wharf and rushed home for a quick change before the ceremony. *Lerina* was then under the command of Captain Fred Dark of Instow. It was warmly concluded in the *Ilfracombe Chronicle* item entitled Bridegroom's Dash that '. . . the bridegroom was in charge of the engine and drove with a good heart'.

In the late summer of 1939, a day-return fare to Lundy by *Lerina* from Instow cost ten shillings, and an official handbill advertising her sailings during the first three period weeks of September showed that there would be trips on Tuesdays, Thursdays and Saturdays. Each departure from Instow Quay was preceded by a connecting departure fifteen minutes earlier from Appledore (Bidna Wharf) operated by small boat to take passengers out to *Lerina* at her River Torridge mooring off Instow. The pattern was very simple, and typically a morning departure from Instow at, say 8 a.m. would give Lundy excursionists about six or seven hours ashore with arrival back at Instow at about 7 p.m. on the evening tide. The list of ticket sales outlets for her sailings was impressive, and as well as Captain Dark taking bookings at his home at 2 Elm Terrace, Instow reservations could also be made at Mr Robert Helson of 2 Silver Street, Appledore; Harpers Library at Bideford; Mr A E Blackwell at Instow; or the office of the Lundy & Atlantic Coast Air Lines, Ltd. at the North Devon Aerodrome, Heanton Court Barnstaple. This

1939 sailing bill for the LERINA.
AUTHOR'S COLLECTION

handbill also referred to the availability of *Lerina* for hire for special trips, excellent accommodation at the Manor Farm Hotel on the island, and lobster luncheons at three shillings.

The fortunes of Lundy's mailboat were soon to be disturbed and *Lerina* was hired with her crew for war use in June 1940. By the end of 1940 the Admiralty had set up coastal patrolling arrangements and these featured a number of vessels, mainly Bideford fishing craft, using a permanent mooring set up in the bay at Lundy as their base, joined by *Lerina* and Fred Dark and his mate and engineer. She was still permitted to carry passengers and stores to the island, and other vessels which supplemented her were the *T.H.E.* (a Brixham sailing trawler motorised before the war and whose initials stood for Teresa, Harriet, Edith, the daughters of an earlier owner) and *Annie Vesta*, locally owned by a Mr Badcock. Neither of these two vessels was a stranger to Lundy having occasionally relieved *Lerina* in peacetime. Initially the Ministry of War Transport were prepared to pay monthly for the use of *Lerina* as an Auxiliary Patrol Vessel, but the Admiralty soon directed that they required to buy her, and the offer of £2,000 was accepted by Mr Harman with the proviso that he would be able buy back his vessel when the war was over.

The Barnstaple Custom House shipping registry entry for *Lerina* was closed on 25 April 1942 and it was recorded that the vessel had been acquired on behalf of His Majesty, and that under a direction from the Chief Registrar of Shipping dated 24 April 1942 registry was no longer required. According to Mr Gade's memoirs her naval use continued until around 1944 but her Bolinder engine received poor treatment from a succession of naval engineers during hostilities and she was put into the Small Vessel Pool in the River Torridge, anchored in one of the creeks above Appledore. Drying out at each ebb, she heeled over on her port side each tide and developed structural weaknesses. She was repurchased by Harman around 1947 for the sum of £400 but, despite remedial work, was never again quite the vessel she had been.

Captain Fred Dark died suddenly of heart failure in the middle of summer 1942, and was greatly missed. The Dark family connection with Lundy, through father and son, dated back to the 1870s, and his death as an elderly man still at work was thought to have been as a result of his vigorous devotion to duty. Having been relieved of the command of *Lerina* in the summer of 1941 he had been appointed R.N. Pilot for the Taw and Torridge estuary. His duties included taking all naval craft, even those as small as motor launches,

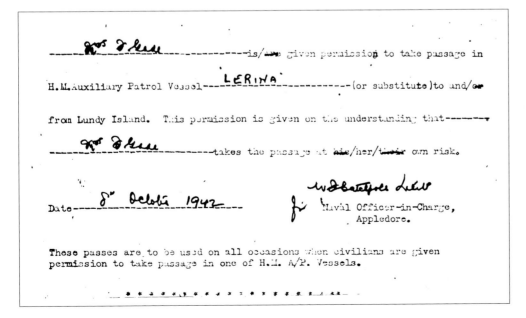

A Naval pass for Mrs Gade to travel aboard H. M. Auxiliary Patrol Vessel LERINA during the Second World War.

The Belgian trawler DE HEILIGE FAMILIE pictured during the 1950s after she had returned to Belgium having served Lundy in the later years of the Second World War.
CORVELEYN, OSTEND

out over the Bideford Bar and similarly meeting all naval craft entering the estuary. In a fulsome testimony to his skills, Gade emphasised how Appledore and similar small ports bred a class of man wholly able to handle sailing vessels and very few of whom followed any other profession than going to sea. Fred Dark's standing amongst his own kind was such that he had a bold reputation for going out to sea, combined with a very shrewd judgement of the weather, and for never being flurried. With his death an era ended, even if his vessel *Lerina* was to struggle on for a little while longer yet.

Little is documented of the exact nature of all the naval manoeuvres in the Torridge area affecting Lundy during the Second World War but information from Belgium came to light regarding one vessel which served Lundy between 1942 and 1945. The Belgian trawler *De Heilige Familie* (The Holy Family) was built

by Boelwerf at Temse in 1936, numbered 0.124 and measured 125 GRT. This vessel left Belgium in May 1940 as the Germans invaded, and arrived in Dartmouth on 22 May. She subsequently became a harbour auxiliary, and served Lundy in lieu of *Lerina* until she finally returned to Belgium in September 1945 to resume a trawling career which lasted until 1971. After a lengthy period of lay-up she was struck from the Belgian Register of fishing vessels in 1976, and scrapped in 1990.

Paddle steamer sailings to Lundy by P. & A. Campbell Ltd. had ended in September 1939 and were not resumed until 1949. In the period before that, in summer 1948, *Lerina* was duly put back into service and Mr Harman engaged the services of a new skipper for her, Captain Wilson, and also took on a young Trevor Davey as mate. The base for the Lundy mailboat now became Bideford rather than Instow. In the absence of any ability to deal with volumes of excursionists from paddle-steamers on the island at this time, plus the fact that Mr Gade had nominally retired from Lundy and gone to work at the Hartland Quay Hotel, only limited numbers of people could visit the island. The setting up of the Lundy Field Society in 1946 stimulated the interests of naturalists who required access by boat as no regular air services then operated. One vessel that made the crossing from Ilfracombe for parties was the fishing boat *Girl Joyce*, a Cornish lugger skippered by the coxswain of the Ilfracombe lifeboat. The Secretary of the Lundy Field Society noted in 1949, when it

.A. E. BLACKWELL
PHONE INSTOW

D 28

LUNDY

•

DAY TRIP *per m.v. "Lerina"*

RETURN FARE
including 10/- ONE PASSENGER
embarking
and disembarking at Instow and Lundy and landing fee at Lundy.

	ketch-rigged, raked stem, cruiser-stern
Tonnage	17.76 gross registered tons (subsequently 19.08 after acquisition for Lundy service)
Build	Carvel, wood fishing and cargo, two bulkheads
Length	46.8 ft.
Breadth	16.65 ft.
Depth	5 ft 5 ins. (in hold) , length of engine-room 12.5 ft.
Machinery	One engine, internal combustion, vertical, 4-stroke cycle, geared diesel, British 1949, Ruston & Hornsby, Lincs., five cylinders 5³/₈ ins. diameter, 8 ins. stroke, 100 BHP, 7.22 NHP, 118 IHP, 8 knots est. speed

Of strictly functional appearance, *Lundy Gannet* lacked any kind of provision for passenger comfort, but was equipped with a new five cylinder Kelvin diesel engine of 90 h.p. Minus the fishing-gear with which she had originally been designated as a 'long-liner', she was capable of carrying twelve passengers and was deemed by Mr Gade to be well suited to her new role. She had been repainted, and now sported a green hull with black bulwarks and red boot-topping. A new, stronger mast had yet to be fitted to adapt her better for cargo-handling at Lundy, and this was duly selected and installed the following autumn. On her positioning voyage to the Bristol Channel she had an uneventful trip, calling en-route at Dover, Weymouth, Falmouth, Newlyn and Clovelly. A retired trawler skipper, Dan Crawford, brought her round from Scarborough with her new skipper Trevor Davey.

Lundy Gannet made her first appearance at Lundy on the Sunday night before her maiden voyage to Lundy from Bideford, which took place on Wednesday 27 June 1956, and was duly recorded in the *Bideford Gazette*. Amid the bustle and traffic noise of the busy Bideford Quay, the Revd R. C. Dixon, Vicar of Appledore and Priest in Charge of Lundy,

blessed the vessel in its new mission. Good for the carriage of 20 tons of cargo, *Lundy Gannet* had a service speed of about eight knots, similar to *Lerina*. Mail from the island had been carried by the air service, but since 1 June, the postal address was amended back to Lundy Island, Bristol Channel, c/o GPO, Bideford. Busy storing away the cargo of stores – ranging from pig food to drums of Calor gas, wash tubs and groceries to numerous cases of liquid refreshment for the thousands of visitors who visited the island aboard White Funnel Fleet steamers – was Peter Lecky, who came of a Channel Islands seafaring family. After 16 years Merchant Navy service, including the training ship *Worcester*, and experience as a Lieutenant in the Royal

With sails stowed LUNDY GANNET *here lies motionless alongside Bideford Quay with the reflection of the bridge visible.*
GRAHAME FARR COLLECTION, COURTESY OF NIGEL COOMBES

These two snaps from 1957 depict a different angle of life on Lundy, namely the method of shipping sheep off the island involving a small boat, plenty of manpower and doubtless lots of physical effort. Getting them on board LUNDY GANNET for the voyage across to Bideford would have presented a further challenge.
MYRTLE TERNSTROM
COLLECTION

Naval Reserve, he described himself smilingly as deckhand.

Albion Harman told the *Bideford Gazette* reporter that it was planned that *Lundy Gannet*, as far as practicable, should go to the island nearly every fine day in the summer. Combined with her operation as cargo and passenger boat, she would be also available for bookings by parties wishing to go to the island from Bideford or elsewhere, and it was intended to do small scale fishing, to include the famous lobsters and crayfish of Lundy among the catches. She would link the island with Devon, and go fishing in the winter. He added that now they had the new link, he planned to visit the island regularly. A small party was held on the island on that Wednesday night to celebrate the inauguration of the new service.

Myrtle Langham travelled out to Lundy on the new vessel shortly after its introduction to the route and described how she left Bideford Quay at 4 p.m. on 4 August 1956 with a full complement of passengers, including Mr Harman. Arrival at Lundy was at 7.10 p.m. after 'a somewhat choppy crossing', and she noted that the Lundy launch which came out to meet *Lundy Gannet* was manned by the farm bailiff. She felt that *Lundy Gannet* was a fine boat, although 'it danced a little'. On the following day, at Mr Harman's invitation,

there was a cruise around the island in fine weather on *Lundy Gannet*, for most of the folk then staying on Lundy.

As the Harman family ownership of Lundy continued during the 1950s and into the 1960s little changed as regards communications with the outside world, and publicity material produced for intending visitors bore a remarkable similarity to pre-war advertising. One can imagine Mr Gade having a new pamphlet produced based on the previous one, pausing only to update details. In this case, though, the amendments were more fundamental as the name of the vessel had changed. Being Bideford-based the new vessel *Lundy Gannet* had, of course, severed the long-standing link that her fishing-boat forebear *Lerina* had had with Instow in pre-war years, and sailing days were advertised at slightly more frequent intervals than in the past. Significantly, the tidal constraints of Bideford now made sailing times more inflexible than had been the case before. Compare this delightful image in 1956 with that from the 1920s, when Lundy had been branded as 'Nature's Unspoilt Isle' the message here was indeed a subtle one and, headed 'The Island of Romance' was definitely not aimed at any form of mass market:

A kingdom in itself, free from the trammels of bye-laws and regulations, it has a peculiar was much as had been envisaged by Mr Smith-Cox, P. & A. Campbell Ltd.'s long-serving Managing Director who, in 1969, had had the foresight to negotiate the exclusive ten-year agreement for his company to serve Lundy excursion sailing needs. If each season from 1972 onwards appeared to have a similarity to the previous one, the underlying situation was not quite so simple, however, as the management of P. & A. Campbell Ltd. nurtured a vision – an entirely reasonable one which reflected the desire for long-term survival – to position themselves as the year-round operator to Lundy. As other activities in the upper Bristol Channel had dwindled, Lundy sailings were accounting for a higher proportion of P. & A. Campbell Ltd.'s earnings, It did not take much perspicacity on the part of the Board of P. & A. Campbell Ltd. to realise that, looked at from an accounting viewpoint, the operation by the Landmark Trust of *Polar Bear* on a service solely based around serving the modest needs of Lundy was a relatively expensive commitment, with considerable overheads and little income. Why not, reasoned the joint Managing Directors Clifton Smith-Cox and Tony McGinnity, think in terms of a passenger and cargo vessel that could combine the seasonal excursion role

POLAR BEAR featured in a charismatic Lundy stamp issue, designed by John Dyke, for Christmas 1976.
VICTOR GRAY COLLECTION

with fulfilling the island's basic freight requirements, and thus provide the year-round link with one vessel instead of two, and thus commensurately lower both overheads and running costs?

Rather surprisingly to some onlookers, *Balmoral* was joined by a fleetmate in 1977. A vessel had become available, in the shape of the 1956-built *Scillonian (II)*, which since her introduction to the far west had provided the dependable basic passenger and cargo link between Penzance and St Marys on the Isles of Scilly, and which in the mid-1970s was nearing replacement. An understanding between her owners, the Isles of Scilly Steamship Company Ltd. and P. & A. Campbell Ltd. had been reached, that the latter would purchase

If one did not see POLAR BEAR tied up at Ilfracombe, then there was a good chance she had crossed to Lundy. POLAR BEAR and BALMORAL are seen anchored in close proximity and a launch is about to go out to them from the landing-stage.
AUTHOR

Scillonian (II) once her successor *Scillonian (III)* had entered service and settled down to the route. This duly happened, rather later than initially expected, but early in 1977 the White Funnel Fleet doubled in size as *Balmoral* was joined by the erstwhile Isles of Scilly vessel. Of broadly comparable dimensions, *Scillonian (II)* was, after a short time, renamed *Devonia*. She retained her white Isles of Scilly Steamship Co. Ltd. hull colours in her first year as a P. & A. Campbell Ltd. ship, but now carried the famous Campbell pennant together with a newly-repainted white funnel. At the time of her acquisition by P. & A. Campbell Ltd. no formal agreement about the future shape of Lundy services had then been reached and the deployment found for *Devonia* that year was mainly the operation of passenger cruise services on the River Thames, in the Silver Jubilee year. In 1977 then, *Balmoral* had maintained the P. & A. Campbell Ltd. presence around the whole of the Bristol Channel for six seasons since 1972.

After P. & A. Campbell Ltd. had acquired their second vessel in 1977, plans were drawn up for the conversion of *Devonia* to make her more suitable for her intended Bristol Channel combined excursion and Lundy supply-boat role. It was planned that part of her forward cargo hold would be converted into passenger accommodation, leaving sufficient capacity available to fulfil Lundy's cargo requirements. Regrettably for P. & A. Campbell Ltd., continuing uncertainty then surrounded the future role of the company and these works were never carried out, leaving the former Isles of Scilly passenger/cargo vessel essentially in her as-built form. No agreement about the future of Lundy transport had yet been reached between the Landmark Trust and P. & A. Campbell Ltd., so *Devonia* remained unconverted, and thus not particularly attractive for a pure coastal excursion vessel role.

Whilst the Landmark Trust-controlled *Polar Bear* steadfastly maintained her regular mail, passenger and cargo year-round sailings from Ilfracombe, the White Funnel Fleet handbill for Ilfracombe sailings for the period

SCILLONIAN (II) was built for a tough life on the Penzance-Isles of Scilly link and her flared bow protecting her twin forward cargo-holds gave her a most distinctive appearance. She remained unconverted during her brief career as P. & A. Campbell Ltd.'s DEVONIA, during 1977-80. She is seen here arriving at Ilfracombe on an excursion in 1978, during the period when she and BALMORAL both operated to Lundy, giving the island a very frequent excursion service.
AUTHOR

Sunday 30 July to Monday 28 August 1978 was now a more substantial affair than in previous years, as the frequency of excursion sailings from Ilfracombe to Lundy and elsewhere was greatly increased by the extra availability of *Devonia* alongside *Balmoral*. The Lundy service, taking on average 1 hour 40 minutes from Ilfracombe, was advertised on a regular basis every Tuesday and Thursday, as well as most Sundays and Mondays. At a day-return fare of £4.90 a total of 18 day excursions were offered between 1 and 27 August, perhaps the most frequent P. & A. Campbell Ltd. service that Lundy had ever had. The majority of these sailings were taken by *Devonia*, her deeper draught making her more suited to the down-channel runs. At this time Birnbeck Pier at Weston was still in use and together with Penarth calls, the upper Channel trips tended to need the shallower draught of *Balmoral* to avoid operational difficulties.

As matters turned out the sought-after agreement with the Landmark Trust was never reached and after 1978 *Devonia* was laid up having failed to deliver satisfactory financial returns under difficult circumstances. Thus *Devonia* was destined to pass into history as the Lundy Packet that never was. *Balmoral*, meanwhile, lingered on for a couple more seasons as the last P. & A. Campbell Ltd. ship, and *Polar Bear* carried on with her duties from Ilfracombe. There is little doubt that the plan, if implemented, would have been a desirable one from the P. & A. Campbell Ltd. point of view, and would doubtless have ensured that the company survived for rather longer than it did. Little changed on Lundy as *Polar Bear* continued her routine voyages although her running costs must have been an area of concern for the Landmark Trust who still remained dependent on P. & A. Campbell Ltd. to bring excursionists across.

Looking back, *Polar Bear* can perhaps be associated with a particular set of circumstances and personalities, namely the changed requirements of Lundy in the early-1970s once the island had passed into National Trust ownership. The appointment of the new Agent, Ian Grainger, took place a couple of

years later, in 1971, the year in which *Polar Bear* was acquired. The successor to Mr Grainger, Colonel Bob Gilliat, arrived on Lundy in 1978 and perhaps naturally had differing views about how the island shipping ought to be arranged. In addition to the change in personnel, the needs of the island would have been changing as public awareness of Lundy increased and more holiday properties for letting on the island were completed, and tourism thus grew. However, decisions regarding the provision of shipping were made collectively rather than by the agent alone.

It was recognised that *Polar Bear* had relatively high running costs for the volumes of cargo then on offer, and the view of Col Gilliat (in a 1970s *Sunday Telegraph* article) was that it was sensible to contain the costs of servicing Lundy without sacrificing any of its inherent character. He noted that Lundy did nor receive any subsidy for its shipping link with the mainland, unlike various Scottish offshore islands, and said he hoped the tourist season on Lundy could be extended, and that more staying visitors could be attracted.

Whilst the days of *Polar Bear* might have been numbered, *Balmoral* soldiered on in 1979, continuing to take passengers to Lundy in the established pattern. The economics of running her were not improving though, and after the close of the season Mr Smith-Cox was obliged to serve notice to the Landmark Trust that P. & A. Campbell Ltd. would not to be able to continue to commercially provide the excursion link in 1980. This arguably posed a dilemma for the Landmark Trust. On the one hand, it was still possible to contemplate the original plan for *Devonia* to take on the all-year Lundy role, had a suitable financial and operational framework been identified which suited the interests of both parties. On the other hand, it had still seemed expedient for P. & A. Campbell Ltd. to persevere with *Balmoral* for excursion work as finding the money to rebuild *Devonia* now seemed less of a viable proposition. *Devonia* thus remained laid-up at Bristol, never to sail again commercially as a White Funnel ship.

Nonetheless a new framework was found in 1980 by which *Polar Bear* continued as the island mailboat. A new company, White Funnel Steamers Ltd., was formed to handle 1980 excursion operations using just *Balmoral*, the key co-directors of which were John Smith of the Landmark Trust and Mr Smith-Cox of P. & A. Campbell Ltd., risk now being shared by both parties. On the face of it, little appeared to change and *Balmoral* sailed in the traditional White Funnel colours whilst daily life for the coaster *Polar Bear* remained unchanged. Publicity to a smart new format was produced, sailings throughout the Channel being put on to a slightly more regular-pattern of services as tides permitted. To all intents and purposes *Balmoral* sailed on as a White Funnel vessel, much as she had been doing for the previous ten years or so. P. & A. Campbell Ltd. continued to manage the operation from their Bristol Head Office, whilst the Landmark Trust guaranteed the charter fees of the vessel. (P. & A. Campbell Ltd. was a subsidiary of European Ferries Limited, albeit run locally, but the approval of the parent company had been sought and granted for this experimental arrangement with a new subsidiary company.)

The link to Lundy Island from Ilfracombe (and, to a lesser extent, Lynmouth) was given prominence in the 1980 season White Funnel Steamers Ltd. publicity material. Certain features of the programme – *Balmoral's* last Bristol Channel season for some years – were worthy of note. An 'Express Coach & Sea Trip to Lundy' was promoted; this consisted of coaches on Tuesdays and Thursdays from Westward Ho!, Bideford, Barnstaple and Braunton to Ilfracombe in connection with sailings, at fixed times, at a fare of £6.95 day return. A similar promotion was offered from Lynmouth.

The financial results of one season of White Funnel Steamers Ltd. were not deemed successful – attributable at least in part to poor weather adversely affecting takings. Thus, after almost a century of Bristol Channel excursion steamer activity, the days of the once mighty White Funnel Fleet effectively ended when *Balmoral* was laid up in October 1980 and advertised, together with her fleetmate *Devonia*, for sale. The creation of White Funnel Steamers Ltd. as a joint venture for 1980 season operations was a brave attempt to survive and arguably deserved a better fate. Mr Smith-Cox had been involved for almost thirty years, but had reached the point where he wished to retire. The losses of the joint venture were substantial, the Report of Directors accompanying the audited accounts of P. & A. Campbell Ltd. dated 11 May 1981 tersely recording a loss for the year before as being £177,630 after taxation. The Landmark Trust were unimpressed, to say the least, Col Gilliatt being on record as having described the episode as 'a financial disaster' for the island.

It is difficult for anyone with a fond memory of P. & A. Campbell Ltd. steamers to look back and take a wholly rational view of the events of 1981, but it is emphatically the case that this was the year in which events were to precipitate the biggest change to the Lundy excursion scene. The White Funnel Fleet had ceased to operate after 1980 but a few individuals closely associated with the successful operational preservation of the Clyde paddle-steamer *Waverley* had shown interest in rescuing a former Isle of Wight passenger ferry to run in support of the Clyde steamer. *Waverley* had first appeared in the Bristol Channel in 1979, running a few trips with the blessing of P. & A. Campbell Ltd. rather than in direct competition with *Balmoral*.

The former Portsmouth-based Isle of Wight ship was the Denny-built motor vessel *Shanklin* dating from 1951, and initially it was thought she might be put into service – in an unspecified manner – as operational back-up to the paddle-steamer *Waverley*. There was still considered to be a core Lundy excursion sailings market and *Prince Ivanhoe*, as she became, was an obvious vessel to be deployed on Bristol Channel excursion work once it became clear early in 1981 that *Balmoral* operations would not be resumed. A period of uncertainty about the future of Bristol Channel cruising after the poor results of the 1980 White Funnel Steamers Ltd. episode

ended with the announcement early in 1981 that sailings would hopefully commence in May by *Prince Ivanhoe* in the ownership of the Firth of Clyde Steam Packet Co. Ltd. White Funnel Steamers Ltd. had ceased operations, but nonetheless P. & A. Campbell Ltd. continued in business as the local managers of *Prince Ivanhoe*.

What did this mean for the Lundy excursion business? It effectively meant little or no substantive change to the broad pattern of sailings, other than that *Prince Ivanhoe* carried very smart new colours, and seemed very different indeed on board with her comparatively better facilities for passengers than those which *Balmoral* had offered. Timetables were largely similar to that which had been on offer for the previous decade of single-vessel P. & A. Campbell Ltd.operations, namely two or three excursion sailings a week between Ilfracombe and Lundy, with *Polar Bear* quietly carrying out her Ilfracombe-based regular packet duties. The advent of a new excursion ship in the Bristol Channel was an

exciting event and I remember a couple of splendid but contrasting Lundy voyages in her in July and August 1981. One was in very lively force 6 or 7 conditions, with many people on board wishing they had not bothered to leave the Quay at Ilfracombe as we veritably hammered our way out to Lundy, with spray everywhere, although we enjoyed calmer conditions on the return. The other was in superb, beautiful sunny conditions where one could think that even if the days of the White Funnel Fleet were over this was a more than an acceptable substitute. That was on 2 August 1981, on a sailing from Portishead and Penarth to Ilfracombe and Lundy.

It was too good to last, perhaps. The following day the devastating news broke that *Prince Ivanhoe* whilst cruising off Gower had hit a submerged object off Port Eynon, been ripped open below the waterline and then deliberately run aground in order to get passengers safely ashore in what was recorded as a very efficient life-saving exercise. The accident happened at low water, and a few

PRINCE IVANHOE ran an excursion from Penarth and Ilfracombe to Lundy on Sunday 2 August 1981. The weather was delightful and she lay at anchor after arrival off Lundy looking absolutely splendid, representing what excursionists hoped would be the beginning of a new era of Bristol Channel sailings after the sad demise of the White Funnel Fleet of P. & A. Campbell Ltd. in 1980. The next day she was lost off Port Eynon, on the coast of Gower.
AUTHOR

hours later everyone was safely ashore but *Prince Ivanhoe* was virtually submerged, wrecked. The Bristol Channel, at a stroke, lost its exciting new excursion ship and Lundy lost its seasonal excursion passenger link.

The situation now was desperate as the basic means of transporting the bulk of the passengers to Lundy either on day-excursions or for holidays in the expanded range of holiday cottages had suddenly collapsed. But Lundy would have been much worse off had the initiative not been taken to experiment with the provision of a helicopter service to the island. Thus, access to Lundy was not solely restricted to the limited numbers that *Polar Bear* could carry, but the future now looked rather different without the availability of a dedicated Bristol Channel excursion vessel. In effect, the point had now been reached where a new Lundy dual-purpose vessel was regarded as virtually essential if island tourism interests were to be safeguarded. But it was five more years before this final transition was made, and in the meantime Lundy persevered with the combination of *Polar Bear* and helicopter services, supplemented by a few fleeting appearances each summer of *Waverley* on her nomadic tour around Britain. This seemed an acceptable balance to satisfy demand for access to Lundy whilst helicopter services were permitted, but matters were not to remain like this indefinitely.

At this point it is appropriate to retrace our steps and briefly examine what could have happened from the island perspective rather that of P. & A. Campbell Ltd., if agreement had ever been reached over the latter becoming the all-year provider of the maritime link between Lundy and Devon. Consideration had been given by the Landmark Trust in the early 1970s to an upgrade of *Polar Bear* to equip her with passenger-carrying capacity for over one hundred passengers. Although identified then as being technically feasible, this was not pursued as there was no threat then to the continuation of White Funnel Fleet excursion services. As has been observed, *Polar Bear* took over the role which *Lundy Gannet* had carried out, but her running costs were clearly greater. The notice of withdrawal of White Funnel Fleet services after the 1979 season prompted a reconsideration of this upgrade, in addition to which the Landmark Trust sought to ascertain the indicative price of a new, purpose-built bow-loading dedicated island supply vessel. At around one and a quarter million pounds this was not pursued, nor was the *Polar Bear* enhancement, and the compromise reached was that *Balmoral* ran under the guise of White Funnel Steamers Ltd in 1980.

A Report prepared in 1981-2 by Colonel Gilliat considered very thoroughly the options for Lundy shipping following the loss of *Prince Ivanhoe*, and the question of a rebuild of *Polar Bear* was again evaluated, this time more thoroughly. Two issues were quite clear; the sound condition of *Polar Bear* was such that a refit was technically quite viable, from the point of view of her general condition and thickness of hull-plating. But with a payload of around 100 passengers (more were possible, but at the expense of a reduction in cargo capacity) the economics of her operations at reasonable fare-levels would have been marginal.

Whatever the conclusion then drawn by the Landmark Trust, no rebuilding took place and, for a few more years helicopter services continued to fill the gap. John Puddy was appointed by the Landmark Trust and installed as Agent by 1984 after Col. Gilliat had retired, and before the decision was made to search for a secondhand vessel to fulfil the needs of the island, further consideration was given to the construction of a brand-new vessel. This time, the Naval Architects Burness-Corlett prepared full General Arrangement plans for a 30m vessel, fairly conventional in appearance and not of bow-loading type. Whether or not this might have come to fruition is uncertain and the next chapter deals with the solution that was found following the urgent necessity for a quick solution after helicopter flights were banned in 1985. But before moving on to the earnest search for a new breed of Lundy Packet to cater for all the island's requirement, one major event in the career of *Polar Bear* as the 'Lundy Packet' remains to be documented.

Lest it be thought that five years seems a long time in which to take basic transportation decisions it should be remembered that there was no immediate or obvious solution to the problem caused by the demise of excursion steamer sailings. The vulnerability of Lundy to its dependency on sea-transport was emphasised when, early in John Puddy's reign as Agent, he had to deal with the situation caused by an accident incurred by *Polar Bear* when she was in collision off the North Devon coast in thick fog with the Gibraltar-registered coaster *Arosia*. One local paper reported thus, on 15 July 1983:

Collision severs Lundy's sea link

Lundy's supply ship the Polar Bear, damaged in a collision in thick fog last night, could be laid up for some days while repairs are carried out. If that happens, the island's main link with the mainland would be lost and islanders would have to make alternative arrangements for vital supplies.

The 396-ton former icebreaker [*sic*] was still in Ilfracombe harbour today where she was escorted by the town's lifeboat last night. A surveyor will be inspecting the damaged vessel today and the Polar Bear's skipper Mr Denver Scoines says he should know then how long repairs will take. 'We've got a hole below the deck line and the bows are stove in on the port side. Personally, I would think we would have to be out of commission for a while' he said.

The collision happened about two miles west of Morte Point in a thick fog-bank. Three lifeboats – Clovelly, Appledore and Ilfracombe – and a helicopter from RAF Chivenor were called out, but fortunately the Polar Bear was only holed above the water line. The other vessel, the 496-ton Arosia, was not badly damaged and continued on its passage to Rotterdam. The Polar Bear was carrying nine passengers and four crew when the collision happened. 'We'd been in the fog for about half an hour. I saw it just before the collision, it loomed up and then we just did what we had to do' said Captain Scoines.

Local marine engineer John Shearn was called on to patch up the damage in order to make the coaster safe to proceed to a drydock for full repairs, and *Polar Bear* remained under repair well into late August 1983. In addition to this inconvenience, Lundy had to also cope with a water shortage and supplies were rationed.

A different issue arose later that year, when it emerged that Bideford was vying to recover its position as the mainland port for Lundy, it having been estimated that the local value of the island's trade with the mainland was then around £150,000 per year. A report prepared for Torridge District Council was said to contain details of the financial inducement that would be needed to tempt the Lundy interests to revert to the traditional mainland port location, by means of reduced harbour dues and pilotage charges. In November 1983 *Polar Bear* made a trial sailing from Bideford with a party of Torridge District officials and councillors on board. The allocation of a well-sited berth close to the town centre was envisaged, which would mean the loss of a small number of town parking spaces, but the Council estimated that any loss of harbour dues from fishing boats would be compensated for by a transfer payment from their Environment Committee budget. Tom Frankland, the Torridgeside Chief Executive went on to say that the Council would assist if in the future *Polar Bear* needed replacement. Wendy Puddy, speaking on behalf of her husband stated that Bideford was a good idea for Lundy as the ship would provide a closer link with helicopter services then operating out of Hartland as well as noting that, administratively, Lundy was part of Torridge

District. At that point the Bideford faction hoped to make the transfer effective from as early as January 1984, but the matter was not settled straightaway and *Polar Bear* did not switch from Ilfracombe until mid-1984. This then left Ilfracombe without any Lundy link other than the very occasional *Waverley* calls already mentioned, which the Chairman of the North Devon District Council described as a 'sad blow' for Ilfracombe, having tried to do all that it could to prevent the transfer to the rival port of Bideford.

At this stage, the Landmark Trust was still considering the future of communications between the mainland and Lundy. If the writing had indeed been on the wall for *Polar Bear* as early as 1978 it was now the case that, six years later, no new excursion operator seemed likely to present themselves, although greater passenger capacity at reasonable fare levels was evidently badly needed. The search was on – again – for a new and different type of Lundy Packet to satisfy cargo and passenger needs, and the final part of this story chronicles some of the influences that led to the identification and procurement of the vessel which would fulfil this role.

The era of Ilfracombe as the mainland Lundy Packet port was drawing to a close in 1983, and POLAR BEAR *is seen here leaving the rival port of Bideford on 11 November of that year on a trial run prior to the switch being made.*
FREEMANS PRESS AGENCY

CHAPTER SEVEN

THE NEW ERA
– *OLDENBURG*

When in 1969 the island was advertised for sale we offered rashly to underwrite an appeal to raise the purchase price, and then to restore and run the island if the National Trust would accept ownership. This appeal was successful . . . our 300-ton supply ship, the MS Oldenburg, runs throughout the year from Bideford or Ilfracombe. She carries day visitors as well as those who come to stay and is a handsome, well-appointed vessel which we were lucky to find.
LANDMARK TRUST HANDBOOK (1992 EDITION)

As the 1984 and 1985 seasons unfolded it was not publicly apparent that a search was really on for a new vessel to serve the combined passenger and cargo needs of Lundy. However, *Polar Bear* was still in business, and the mainland base of the Lundy packet had reverted after a comparatively short period of time from Ilfracombe to the Torridge port of Bideford. After the demise of *Prince Ivanhoe* in 1981 the Bristol Channel excursion scene had more or less disappeared, save for the very welcome but fleeting visits by the paddle-steamer *Waverley*; the *Balmoral* was now many hundreds of miles away, serving as a static restaurant ship in Dundee, and not thought likely to ever sail again. *Devonia* had also been sold out of P. & A. Campbell Ltd. ownership, and subsequently underwent a number of changes of ownership, including operating from South Devon for Torbay Seaways for a period as *Devoniun*, eventually leaving UK waters for the Eastern Mediterranean.

At that time there was no immediately obvious tonnage which could be identified on the UK market to serve the passenger and cargo needs of Lundy. It was still the case that the tidal constraints of the River Torridge led to sailing times often being at anti-social hours, and also subject to any disruptions which might be caused by adverse weather and the notorious Bideford Bar. Helicopter services were not a viable option once flights by single-engined craft over the sea were banned in 1985. Ilfracombe, with its naturally higher potential for day-tripper traffic, had scarcely any connection now with Lundy and at this point it was not entirely clear what was

considered by the Landmark Trust to be the best solution for serving Lundy.

Curnow Shipping, a Cornish company mainly known for its St Helena ocean-liner trade, were consulted by the Landmark Trust to advise on a replacement vessel for *Polar Bear*. The study went beyond just a new vessel, and considered terminal sites too. It was clearly the case that a body of opinion then recognised that Bideford would always be at a permanent disadvantage because of tidal constraints if regularity of sailings at realistic daytime hours was sought. Andrew Bell, Managing Director of Curnow Shipping, had identified what could have been an ideal vessel then available for disposal by Red Funnel Steamers at Southampton, and he described the substance of his company's view:

Our proposal centred on renting the CEGB's unused jetty, originally built to handle coal from South Wales, at Yelland. This would have become Lundy's own terminal with everything from secure parking to covered storage in a warehouse. By locating at Yelland, on all but the lowest Mean Low Water Spring, in a two-weekly tidal cycle on four days a mid-day outward departure sailing could have been established; there would have been none of the confusion over where Oldenburg sailed from and arrived back at. Lundy's Agent said that Yelland's pier was only built to carry cranes' tracks but this could have been cured by load spreading sheets on the quay surface.

The vessel that carried our recommendation, coupled with the Yelland terminal, was Red Funnel's Calshot [of 1964]. In our eyes she was ideal. Although she had a deep draught her hull form was a seaworthy

81

The tug/tender CALSHOT, seen here at Southampton shortly before withdrawal by Red Funnel Steamers , was considered by Curnow Shipping (consultants to the Landmark Trust) as a potentially suitable Lundy packet.
AUTHOR

one, she was in excellent condition, very little was needed to adapt her to Lundy's needs and, most importantly of all she had all the certificates for the route and the Dtp surveyors knew her and liked her. This was the glory not to be.

It should be explained that *Calshot* had been built for Red Funnel Steamers as a tug-tender, that is, a tug, but with generous passenger accommodation for handling liner calls. These took place in the mouth of the Solent and saved steaming time on the big transatlantic liners which could load and offload passengers and mails quickly and then carry on their way to or from the Continent. Constructed as late as 1964 with a very neat appearance she enjoyed a fairly quiet life until withdrawal in 1985, but had been well maintained by her owners. Yelland is not far from Instow, just inside the Taw estuary, although its advantage of reasonably unrestricted access by water might have been seen by some as being offset by a slightly awkward location relative to access by passengers without their own cars. The reference to little adaptation being needed was to do with the need for an on-board crane cargo-handling. But the Curnow Shipping proposal was not taken up and the Landmark Trust opted to look further afield.

The need for a multi-purpose vessel to handle the passengers as well as cargo was now self-evident, especially in view of the significant quantity of high-quality holiday

letting accommodation on the island which led to a predictable peak demand on Saturdays, the changeover day for most properties. But what vessel would be selected to carry out this role? Minimal crewing costs were important, but a degree of comfort was needed by way of substitution for what the White Funnel Fleet steamers had provided. Another, critical requirement was that the new vessel had to be capable of being granted a Class II passenger certificate to run all year round rather than just during the summer, along with being equipped with appropriate cargo handling gear.

The Lundy Agent John Puddy wrote in some detail in 1998 in the journal of the Paddle Steamer Preservation Society *Paddle Wheels* of the search in 1985 for the new island vessel. This account can be summarised here by saying that after enquiries to ship-brokers which yielded numerous responses, mainly relating to vessels lying in Scandinavia and Northern Europe, the range of possibilities warranting examination was narrowed down to seven. Five were inspected in Norway by John Puddy and Barty Smith, a Lundy director, but none appeared suitable. Moving on to Germany, *Oldenburg* was seen at Wilhelmshaven, then in service as a 'butter-boat' carrying numbers of German tourists on short cruises from the German mainland which exploited a legal loophole enabling people to buy quantities of duty-free butter. (Such trips were essentially a variant on duty-free trips where the destination was secondary to the money-saving motive for passengers). Finally, the two moved on to Travemunde where the laid-up *Dyroy* was viewed, which appeared to have potential despite her interior having been partly gutted.

John Puddy recorded how *Oldenburg* was chosen, at the toss of a coin. Doubtless other factors had been considered, but negotiations for her purchase got underway and by November 1985 she had been secured by her new owners to become the most radically different Lundy packet yet. A crew was mustered from England to go and collect her and, after a trying voyage involving both mechanical difficulties and gale-force conditions in the English Channel, *Oldenburg* eventually reached the Bristol Channel and showed herself at Lundy for the first time on 5 December 1985. This was a few days later than envisaged in the press-release entitled *Lundy News* issued in November, which advised that she would arrive off Bideford Quay at 09.00 on Tuesday 3 December for a photo-call before being welcomed by Councillor Wilfred Trace, Chairman of the Torridge District Council and Serena Smith, daughter of the Chairman of the Landmark Trust. The announcement emphasised the necessity for *Oldenburg* as a result of cessation of helicopter flights, and made the point that her larger capacity would enable lower fares to be charged, a day-return reducing from £15.00 (1984 prices) to £11.95, including the £2.00 landing charge then in force. Also mentioned was the plan for *Oldenburg's* thrice-weekly sailings from Bideford to Lundy to be combined with twice-weekly Ilfracombe sailings giving a much better service for Devon holidaymakers wishing to visit or stay on Lundy than in the immediately preceding years.

After lying at Lundy overnight *Oldenburg* proudly proceeded up the River Torridge the next day to her new home port of Bideford, where John Puddy recorded that although tenders from a number of yards had been sought, it had been decided that her refit would take place alongside the Quay using local craftsmen. Much of this effort was directed at reducing fire risks as well as fitting out a new shop and improving safety systems, and was to occupy rather more than the three months or so which had been allowed before a hoped-for Easter 1986 debut. Her Class IIa certificate for winter crewing would necessitate four crew-members – Master, Mate, Engineer and Radio Operator/Deckhand – whilst extra deckhands for Class III summer certification would enable around 250 passengers to be carried rather than 150 in winter (the limit of the seating provided internally) and a huge increase on what earlier Lundy Packets had offered.

Oldenburg had been built in 1958 to operate for the DB German Railways between Harle and the East Frisian island of Wangerooge, on rail-connected services. A

Five Lundy Packets, of differing types, had served Lundy for the century or so before the biggest ever transformation was made in 1986. When built for German Railways service in 1958, OLDENBURG had capacity for 408 passengers and eclipsed her predecessors, most of which could convey no more than a dozen souls. Her neat, trim appearance is well depicted in this view of her in the earlier part of her career.
TOM BAKER COLLECTION

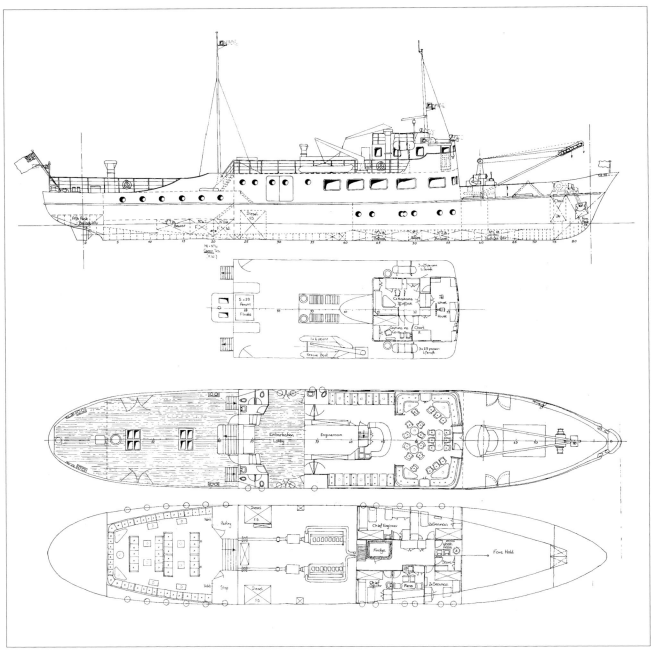

General Arrangement diagram of the OLDENBURG.
IVOR IRELAND COLLECTION

younger half-sister, *Wangerooge*, of slightly greater dimensions but substantially similar appearance, had joined her on the run from 1960. Wangerooge is the easternmost of half a dozen low-lying islands in the shallow seas off the northern German coast, stretching from off Emden eastwards to off Wilhelmshaven, the town of *Oldenburg* (her original port of registry) itself being some way inland. The trip out to Wangerooge by ship took about an hour and a half. When built the passenger capacity of *Oldenburg* was 408, at a tonnage of 312 GRT, although she operated with passengers limited to 310 on the occasional longer runs to Heligoland in the earlier part of her life. She had, by the time she came under Landmark

Trust scrutiny in 1985, been sold by DB and become engaged by her new owners Harle Reederei Warrings of Carolinensiel on 'butter cruises' since 1982.

When her refit was substantially completed, *Oldenburg* was registered at Bideford officially on 2 May 1986 in the ownership of the Lundy Company, John Puddy being named as her Managing Owner. In a category of her own in size when compared to the packets that had preceded her, but more notably on account of her passenger carrying capacity (albeit now markedly less than had been permitted under German registry) the Custom House records give these details:

No.	397660
Port	Bideford
Port no.	2/1986
Type	Motor Ship, Twin-Screw
Where built	Rolandwerft GMBH Bremen-Hemelingen, Bremen 1958
Description	One deck, two masts, not rigged, raked stem, cruiser-stern
Tonnage	294.82 gross tons
Build	Clencher, steel passenger vessel, five watertight bulkheads
Length	132.2 ft.
Breadth	25.65 ft.
Depth	8 ft 7 ins. (in hold) , length of engine-room 23.6 ft.
Machinery	Two engines, b.1958, Motoren-Werke Mannheim, Mannheim F.R.Germany internal combustion, two shafts, eight cylinders 180mm diameter, reciprocating, 260mm stroke, 530 BHP, 11.5 knots est. speed

Oldenburg entered service on Saturday 10 May 1986, rather later than had originally been intended. She sported a hull colour of midnight blue, with white superstructure and a yellow funnel. A trial call had been made at Ilfracombe a few days earlier, on Thursday 1 May. Ideally-sized for her new trade,

Oldenburg's refit had nevertheless been a fairly expensive affair to bring her up to the required standards for UK service, Her two-ton electric crane was retained at this stage, to service the hold of 90 cubic metres capacity. Considerable assistance in the form of European Regional Development Fund grant funding was received, and both the English Tourist Board and the West Country Tourist Board also made contributions to her purchase. Her passenger capacity was then listed as 242 (Class 3) and 130 (Class 2a).

Being a more obviously visible and capacious Lundy Packet than a modified fishing boat, like certain of her forebears, the life and times of *Oldenburg* have already been better documented, and my purpose here is to illustrate the varied ways in which she has been deployed around the Bristol Channel – in addition to servicing Lundy. There was a brief period in the late-1980s when an uneasy balance existed between direct Lundy interests and the newly-reborn Bristol Channel excursion steamer services. These latter, arising phoenix-like in 1986, rather took some observers by surprise, utilising as they did the ex-P. & A. Campbell Ltd. motorship *Balmoral* which remarkably re-entered service after five years of inactivity, and only a matter of weeks apart from the introduction of the smartly-rebuilt *Oldenburg*.

OLDENBURG at Bideford Quay in 1986 before her funnel had been painted yellow.
IVOR IRELAND

As the 1986 season unfolded fares on *Oldenburg* were duly reduced, and a day-return fare cost £11.95 (adults) and £6.00 (children under 16 years old). An adult period return fare cost £22.00. These rates incorporated the £2.00 admission fee to the island. Her basic first year schedule was largely based on Bideford, albeit with a significant number of trips out of Ilfracombe offered as well. Having acquired a new island ship it was only logical that this asset would be used to advantage for Lundy. In offering a fairly frequent and regular pattern, this meant that many Bideford Saturday sailings (the key holiday property changeover day on the island) were, however, inevitably at distinctly anti-social hours. This was as a result of being wholly tide-dependent, for example, with departures from Bideford at 03.30 on Saturday 16 August 1986, and at 02.30 on Saturday 30 August 1986. The absence of any on-board cabin accommodation exacerbated this anti-social attribute of *Oldenburg* sailings in that first season, which to some extent offset the positive aspect to passengers of most sailings being made from the primary base of Bideford. The first basic winter 1986-7 schedule for *Oldenburg* was to run on Mondays, Fridays and Saturdays from Bideford to Lundy.

Perhaps the Landmark Trust, in their calculations, had not seriously expected that seasonal excursion sailings from Ilfracombe to Lundy would ever resume with any kind of significant frequency, but once it became apparent that members of the Paddle Steamer Preservation Society were determined to try and restore what they could of the Bristol Channel excursion services with the *Balmoral* (operated by Waverley Excursions Ltd.), it was inevitable that in some senses *Oldenburg* and *Balmoral* would be competing in a fairly modestly-sized market. Some timetable coordination in that first year was evident, and the two vessels ran independently, on different days, to Lundy. Crucially, this destination for *Balmoral* was now no longer the key feature of the Waverley Excursions Ltd. programmes as it had been up until the end of the P. & A. Campbell Ltd. 1970s era.

One interesting feature of that initial phase of *Oldenburg* operation was that the carriage of passengers on the scenic coastal run between Bideford and Ilfracombe (and vice versa) was then advertised when positioning was taking place, often in the early morning or evening. A first meeting between *Oldenburg* and *Balmoral* occurred at Lundy on Bank Holiday Monday, 26 May 1986, and a little later the paddle-steamer *Waverley* was also in the area so that the first 'Three Ships' meeting took place on Wednesday 18 June 1986. On this occasion, the venerable former P. & A. Campbell Ltd. launch *Westward Ho* tendered to the excursion ships at Lundy (along with one of *Waverley's* boats and *Islander*, the latter having been acquired by the Landmark Trust and based at the island since 1985) but this role was later carried out by an Ilfracombe launch, *African Queen*, which went out to Lundy on days when *Balmoral* was due to call.

The main originating points of up-Channel passengers were Penarth Pier and Portishead, as at this time Clevedon Pier had not been reconstructed. Further west, Mumbles Pier was still in use, but in deteriorating condition. By the later part of the 1986 season, *Polar Bear* could still be seen laid-up at Appledore. The final Lundy excursion call of the season by the paddler *Waverley*, on 4 October 1986, was unable to land passengers owing to adverse weather conditions, and a cruise around the island substituted.

The new Lundy Packet was now seemingly secure in her role and generally met with satisfaction from her passengers, many of whom – it should be said – had a greater concern in getting to the island as painlessly as possible than in any kind of inherent interest in a ferryboat, a mere means to an end in reaching the favoured isle. Her predecessor *Polar Bear*, after a lengthy period of lay-up, was sold late in 1987, and the Barnstaple Shipping Register transactions record that whilst her ownership initially passed from the Lundy Company to the Swanage Brick & Tile Company on 8 September 1987, she then almost immediately passed to the ownership of Cyril and Fitzroy Hyacinth, both seamen, of the Commonwealth country of Dominica, on 11 September 1987, for further trading.

Oldenburg fitted well with the changing requirements for Lundy. She offered adequate catering on-board, crossed at sensible frequencies and was inherently an attractive and fairly economic vessel to operate in terms of crewing. She nevertheless represented a

The first 'Three Ships' event occurred at Lundy on 18 June 1986 when OLDENBURG, WAVERLEY and BALMORAL all met at Lundy for the first time. The Lundy launch ISLANDER is alongside OLDENBURG.
ALAN KITTRIDGE

87

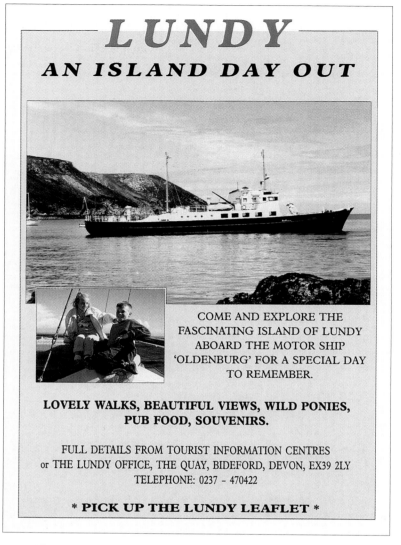

LUNDY
AN ISLAND DAY OUT

COME AND EXPLORE THE
FASCINATING ISLAND OF LUNDY
ABOARD THE MOTOR SHIP
'OLDENBURG' FOR A SPECIAL DAY
TO REMEMBER.

**LOVELY WALKS, BEAUTIFUL VIEWS, WILD PONIES,
PUB FOOD, SOUVENIRS.**

FULL DETAILS FROM TOURIST INFORMATION CENTRES
or THE LUNDY OFFICE, THE QUAY, BIDEFORD, DEVON, EX39 2LY
TELEPHONE: 0237 - 470422

* PICK UP THE LUNDY LEAFLET *

*Advertising showcard for
OLDENBURG.*

significant commitment of capital expenditure by the Landmark Trust to the provision of increased standards of access to Lundy, and was clearly going to have to earn her keep as far as possible. Co-existence was maintained with the sailings offered by *Balmoral*, but as 1987 and 1988 drew on more emphasis was put on Ilfracombe rather than Bideford sailings by *Oldenburg*, from where she offered more convenient mid-morning departure times, could tap a greater number of holidaymakers and still provide a reasonable amount of time on the island. In 1987 a small number of coastal cruises out of Ilfracombe were offered by *Oldenburg*, eastwards towards

the Foreland Point, and of three hours duration

One noteworthy event early in 1988 was the carriage by the Royal Mail Ship *St Helena* of passengers – and the mails – who were stranded on Lundy. The UK-registered liner was returning from South Africa to Avonmouth, and had sought shelter in the lee of Lundy whilst awaiting the tide. The weather had prevented *Oldenburg* from calling at Lundy for some days, and seventeen Christmas visitors to the island had been stranded.

An excursion link between Ilfracombe and Swansea was offered experimentally in 1988 on around a dozen occasions by the Lundy Packet, a new departure for the island interests controlling *Oldenburg* but one which incurred a considerable degree of operating expense relative to passenger demand, and was not subsequently repeated. On some occasions *Oldenburg* simply offered a day-return facility from Ilfracombe to Swansea with maybe four hours or so ashore, but on other days she would position early in the morning to offer a day return trip the other way round for Swansea folk to enjoy a day in Ilfracombe. The day return fare was £9.95, and marketing in Swansea was handled by the South Wales Transport bus company at the Quadrant Bus Station. Although not commercially successful in its own right, this experiment was the beginning of endeavours to operate *Oldenburg* further afield in subsequent years to generate additional income.

Trouble was brewing for Waverley Excursions Ltd. as the 1988 season rolled on, and on Saturday 11 June 1988 an incident occurred which was to have considerable repercussions. Interpretations of the sequence of events varied, but the facts were that the weather turned after *Waverley* had discharged her passengers at Lundy, who ended up being stranded on the island for most of the night until conditions abated sufficiently to allow *Waverley* to return early the following morning to collect them. *Waverley*, in the meantime, carried out another commitment that evening from Ilfracombe, and inevitably some felt that she should have been at least standing by at the anchorage at Lundy Roads for her returning Lundy passengers – irrespective of conditions – rather than leaving the island. Difficulties were inevitably experienced in sheltering such numbers overnight on the island, and the Landmark Trust decided later in the year that Waverley Excursions Ltd. vessels would no longer be allowed to land passengers at Lundy. This ban remained for a while, during the 1989 and 1990 seasons. However, happily for excursionists, discussions took place and the differences of opinion between the Landmark Trust and Waverley Excursions Ltd. were eventually overcome and a new agreement was reached. Waverley Excursions Ltd.'s sailings, albeit only of a fairly occasional nature, were to have been resumed on Saturday 4 May 1991 by *Balmoral*. What should have been her triumphant return to Lundy was sadly thwarted by weather, rough easterly conditions caused the landing to be cancelled, and a round-the-island cruise was substituted instead. But, more importantly, Lundy was now back on the

comprehensive round-Britain map of Waverley Excursions Ltd. sailings, and a worthy Bristol Channel tradition restored as the honour fell to the much-loved paddler *Waverley* to resume calls on Saturday 15 June 1991.

After the initial 1986 season more emphasis was given by *Oldenburg* to providing sailings out of Ilfracombe Harbour at convenient times rather than being totally dependent on the tide at Bideford. In 1989, for example, during the two week period between Saturday 8 and Saturday 22 July inclusive, six sailings were advertised from Ilfracombe and three from Bideford. As if to revive the brief period in the early 1920s when *Lerina* ran to Lundy from Barnstaple – the rival Port to Bideford – a number of trips up the tortuous River Taw passage to Barnstaple's Town Quay have been operated. Two such excursions were advertised in 1988, and two more in 1989. This general pattern persisted for a few more seasons, but considerable navigational difficulties in the shallow waters of the Taw led to these trips being withdrawn

One of WAVERLEY's boats approaching the landing stage at Lundy on 18 June 1986, with OLDENBURG and ISLANDER in the background. ALAN KITTRIDGE

Far from her normal territory. OLDENBURG *seen here passing Purton on the Gloucester Ship Canal en-route from Clevedon to Gloucester on 24 May 1992.* AUTHOR

On one occasion in 1994 OLDENBURG *briefly came experimentally alongside the quay at Clovelly when tidal conditions were favourable. Passengers are normally handled by launch at this attractive location* JOHN LAVINGTON

after the 1994 season. *Oldenburg* had briefly grounded on the 19 September 1993 trip on the River Taw. Friday was the normal off-service day for Oldenburg at this time.

The first ten years, 1986 to 1995, of the life and times of *Oldenburg* can perhaps be conveniently divided into two phases, the first five years representing the establishment of the new order with *Oldenburg* substantively Bideford-based but steadily laying down a pattern of well marketed Ilfracombe Lundy excursions to generate valuable additional revenues for the island. However, by 1991 all was not well financially and it was stated that on an island turnover of £450,000, losses of £130,000 were being incurred, largely attributed to transportation difficulties and costs. Agent John Puddy pointed out (in an article printed in the Lundy Field Society newsletter) that if *Oldenburg* were unable to carry out a landing trip to Lundy on account of easterly winds, and a round-the-island cruise substituted, then losses of around £3,000 per occasion might be incurred as many day-excursionists would not bother to travel if unable to go ashore. 'Lundy has virtually broken everyone who has owned it because of the difficulties of getting there and particularly of landing' said Mr Puddy. A solution was held to lie in the provision of a fixed jetty at Lundy where the ship could tie up virtually irrespective of conditions, offering greater reliability and the bonus of more time ashore, although this major project was actually still some years away. This was despite well-publicised plans in 1987 which would have involved the shipment of concrete blocks manufactured on the mainland out to Lundy to form the basis of such a construction.

In the second half of *Oldenburg's* first decade the themes were positive ones; a form of flag-waving for Lundy has been the promotion of the island by the occasional appearances of *Oldenburg* at unfamiliar locations as she was used to offer enterprising trips to destinations as far afield as Clevedon and Bristol (1991) and Gloucester (1992). The Bristol venture was a novel and enterprising one and represented a conscious effort to increase awareness of what Lundy had to offer. Whilst at Bristol, *Oldenburg* berthed centrally outside the Arnolfini Gallery, at the location previously known as Narrow Quay in the earlier days of Bristol when the commercial port was at its heart of the city. Visitors were invited to meet the Captain and crew, and sample Lundy-brewed ale on board. In addition, a harbour-cruise and river-trip were operated by *Oldenburg*, although foul weather predominated. A nice touch, which illustrated the underlying strength of the inherently complementary and positive relationship between excursion sailings to Lundy and island-controlled packet interests was that Capt Neill, master of the paddle-steamer *Waverley*, piloted *Oldenburg* in the River Avon. The 1992 season marked the beginning of a new style of integrated marketing of sailings with holiday accommodation on Lundy, supported by well designed sales literature which was more widely distributed. The versatility of *Oldenburg* was well displayed when, in May 1992, she traversed the Gloucester and Sharpness Canal to reach Gloucester from Clevedon, making an impressive sight as she glided along the tranquil canal on a sunny day, in contrast to the more lively regular Lundy passage out at sea in the normal working week.

Oldenburg proved her usefulness elsewhere when the Isles of Scilly ferry *Scillonian (III)* experienced mechanical difficulties in April and May 1991. She was briefly chartered by the Isles of Scilly Steamship Company Ltd. to provide relief on the Penzance to St Marys run. From 1994 onwards Clovelly, Minehead and Watchet have also been visited by *Oldenburg*, Clovelly particularly having developed as a regularly featured port of

departure for Lundy. The normal advertised passage time to Lundy on *Oldenburg* from Bideford or Ilfracombe was then two and a quarter hours. From Clovelly a much shorter passage of one and a half hours is offered. In 1994 Clovelly had just seven Lundy trips confined to the high summer season months of July and August, but by 1997 the Clovelly season had stretched out to the May to September period. These trips require *Oldenburg* to be tendered, although she has on one occasion at least cautiously come alongside the picturesque harbour wall at Clovelly. The operation of *Oldenburg* has not been wholly incident-free and an unfortunate grounding in unexpected thick fog in the River Torridge on Saturday 30 October 1993 received a surprising amount of publicity, both locally and nationally, as four pairs of ships wellington-boots were used in turn by passengers to walk across the Torridge river-bed when the tide was out in order to evacuate the ship safely.

OLDENBURG attracted attention when she had the misfortune to run aground in the River Torridge in fog on Saturday 30 October 1993 whilst outward bound to Lundy on an 07.00 departure from Bideford, with 44 passengers on board. The emergency was handled adroitly and she was soon afloat again, undamaged.
FREEMANS PRESS AGENCY

An excellent account of a very interesting day on board *Oldenburg* on 25 July 1994 was provided in *Cruising Monthly* by sub-Editor Brian Kennedy in the October 1994 edition, the inspiration being a rare departure from the ancient Somerset port of Watchet to Lundy, not thought to have been offered since before the Second World War. The Town Crier turned out to see off *Oldenburg* with over 100 excited passengers for a cruise along the Exmoor Coast to Ilfracombe, and thence on to Lundy after a further 160 passengers had been picked up. Disembarkation at Lundy was carried out by the launch *Wendy*, at around 25 passengers per trip to to the Landing Beach, assisted also by the Landmark Trust's then newly-acquired Avon W520 inflatable craft, carrying a further 12 passengers per trip. The island's other launch *Islander* was also deployed on tendering that day. (This vessel has on occasions offered scheduled Clovelly Lundy crossings, and carried the mails.) The

return trip after a good two and a half hours ashore, sufficient to have enabled the rhododendrons and the Old Light to be appreciated, was to Bideford, and after departure at 17.15 for the scenic run back to the North Devon coast and along the River Torridge past Appledore *Oldenburg* made fast at Bideford Quay at 19.30, where coaches were waiting to return passengers to Watchet. The friendliness of the crew was acknowledged, together with the very smart condition of the ship, and Brian Kennedy highly recommended the varied sailings programme of *Oldenburg* to all Coastal Cruising Association members.

A first for *Oldenburg* was an extremely unusual trip from Clevedon Pier to Dunball Wharf, on the River Parrett in Somerset, during June 1998. Padstow trips were also operated in 1998.

An extreme level of disruption to the Lundy service was experienced late in 1996,

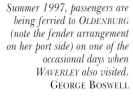

Summer 1997, passengers are being ferried to OLDENBURG *(note the fender arrangement on her port side) on one of the occasional days when* WAVERLEY *also visited.*
GEORGE BOSWELL

The former residence of the Heaven family, Millcombe, functioned as a hotel in the 1980s but subsequently became one of the larger self-catering properties on the island, suitable for 12 guests in great style and comfort. Oldenburg is seen at her anchorage on a pleasant sunny day in 1996.
AUTHOR

on 29 November, when *Oldenburg* was forced to run for Bristol as very strong gales made Bideford unreachable on the return from Lundy to the mainland.

We come now to 1999, the year in which probably the greatest change ever in voyaging to Lundy took place, when the project to build a pier finally reached a conclusion. We have seen how earlier packets developed the ability to land their essential cargoes at various points around Lundy if easterlies made the landing-beach untenable, exemplified particularly by *Lerina* under the skilled hands of Captain Dark between the wars. The desire for a pier was long-standing, to overcome the precarious transhipments between ship and small boat and the uncertainty of the ever-changing weather, and perhaps above all else to obviate the need for the manpower of the small island to have to spend so much time at the beach away from their other tasks when mailboat day came round.

The intention had been in 1987 that the pier would have been constructed as a solid, concrete affair with concrete blocks prefabricated on the mainland at Fremington, shipped to Lundy and then keyed together and filled, on a prepared bed. The Landmark Trust were reported as having purchased the

200 ton coaster *Dawnlight I* from the Scottish company Glenlight Shipping, for a sum of £55,000 and the whole scheme – to include a road to gain access from the landing beach further around the bay to the cove, at sufficient height above spring tide height was initially costed at around £1.3m. The Royal Marines at Instow were to have cooperated in this venture, as representing good practical training in a sometimes harsh maritime environment. Regrettably, the estimated costs escalated (to more like £2m), so the scheme was shelved and the coaster disposed of.

But ten years later a new design was prepared and the decision taken in 1998 to proceed, with the assistance of grants. The first phase of the project necessitated the reinforcement of the extended Beach Road, in order that access to the primary work site could be gained. Construction of a new design of piled pier began in earnest in 1999, it having been assessed that this type of construction would be less damaging to the sensitive marine environment as well as less costly. The method chosen for its construction involved drilling down about 5m to secure the 1000mm diameter steel piles and then placing precast concrete members horizontally to form the gently-sloping deck, to cater for the wide

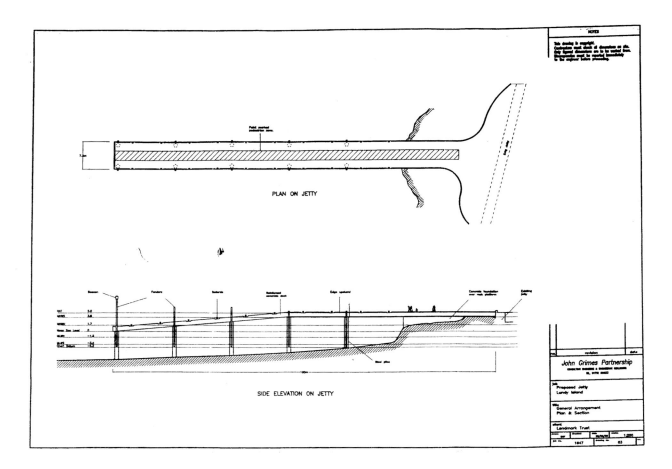

PLAN ON JETTY

SIDE ELEVATION ON JETTY

*General arrangement diagram
of the landing jetty at Lundy.*
COURTESY
LANDMARK TRUST

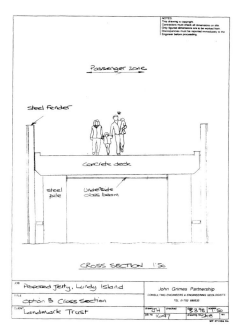

tidal range prevalent throughout the Bristol Channel. The precast concrete components came from Pembroke Dock in South Wales, by barge, but much of the building material was shipped out through Bideford by *Oldenburg*. A rig was brought in from Belgium to deal with the drilling, and by summer 1999 a recognisable pier of functional form had taken shape, within the budget of around one million pounds, built by the construction company Taylor Woodrow. Extreme care had to be taken to minimise disturbance to the seabed when drilling operations took place, to protect and safeguard the Marine Nature Reserve status of Lundy.

The weather inevitably caused delays, as did a rig-collapse, but the first use made of Lundy's long awaited new pier was by *Oldenburg* on the day of the solar eclipse, August 11 1999, when she called en-route on a very special sailing from Bideford to off

Padstow, to reach the zone of totality, and collected a handful of holidaymakers staying on Lundy. Construction work had not quite finished then, and *Oldenburg* berthed only intermittently at the new pier during the next three weeks, but the construction contract was due to end after August, and thus Wednesday 1 September 1999 became the first official day of use of the new pier. *Oldenburg* arrived, without ceremony at midday, very properly from her Torridge home-port of Bideford which she had left at 10.00, in perfect weather, with a very good load of 214 passengers on board. The Lundy landing craft *Shearn* was not used after this and was disposed of.

The other key event of 1999 had been a major refit for *Oldenburg*, together with the installation of new engines, which occupied most of the first three months of the year and was carried out at Appledore. Her exterior appearance was improved by a new steel awning above the aft deck, which replaced a

rather temporary looking tent-like affair, and of rather greater importance to many passengers was the ability of the new Cummins engines to shorten the typical passage time, the journey from Bideford reducing from two and a quarter hours to more like just two hours as a result in an increase in speed from about 11 to 13 knots. Her interior was upgraded too, one of the most obvious enhancements being a complete re-upholstering of the aft saloon. Her passenger certificate now declared her capacity as 267 passengers (Class III) and 151 (Class IIa). Her crew complement is now eight in summer and six in winter, comprised of Captain, Mate, two in the Engineering department all year-round, Information Officer, Barman, Shopkeeper and Buffet Attendant. The four latter roles are combined into two in the winter.

By sheer chance, I happened to be on board *Oldenburg* on that historic first day of September 1999 in order to make the most of

Construction work underway on the new pier for Lundy in early 1999
TOM BAKER COLLECTION

OLDENBURG at the new pier on the first official day of use on 1 September 1999.
AUTHOR

Later the same day, BALMORAL arrived from Swansea and boosted the sense of occasion as she became the first excursion steamer to use the new pier, on the other berth. OLDENBURG is scarcely visible behind BALMORAL.
AUTHOR

a day on Lundy with more time ashore than can be offered by a trip from a more distant up-Channel port such as Penarth by *Balmoral* or *Waverley*. A double historic occasion occurred as *Balmoral* was also due that day at Lundy from Swansea, and clearance had been given a few days earlier by the Landmark Trust to Waverley Excursions Ltd. for the passenger motorship to come alongside the new pier for the very first time. Thus, at 14.00 the pier was occupied by the Lundy Packet *Oldenburg* on the 'inner berth' (closer to Rat Island) and the excursion steamer *Balmoral* on the 'outer berth', a truly remarkable sight after centuries of landings by small boat.

Captain Roger Hoad of *Oldenburg* had been closely consulted over the design of the new pier, and saw the project through to its conclusion before moving on to become the Torridge River Pilot in September 1999. The opinion of the new pier by the Captain of *Balmoral*, Steve Colledge, was later succinctly expressed in just one word – 'excellent'. It often used to take up to a couple of hours to get a typical load of between 200 and 300 passengers ashore by launch, depending on

the capacity and number of launches available, whereas ten minutes or so alongside the new pier now suffices to discharge all passengers. A possibility offered by the pier for excursionists is that it is now feasible to provide a round Lundy cruise as an alternative to time ashore.

A perfect day on Lundy thus ended when I was able to photograph *Balmoral* making her first departure from the new pier at 17.30, her passengers having had around three hours ashore that day rather than just the hour or two at most that would typically have been available between landings by launch. *Oldenburg* passengers were advised to be ready at the pier to embark at 18.40, for a very punctual 19.00 departure across to Bideford. A glorious passage, in the setting sun, took us over the Bar and into the River Torridge with scarcely any sensation to worry the less seaworthy on board, and after a leisurely sail past Appledore and Instow – home of the Darks, father and son and *Gannet* and *Lerina* – we were alongside at Bideford Quay promptly at 21.00. The Lundy Packet had arrived home safely.

Oldenburg seen from Instow, passing Appledore. The steps in the foreground are those of Instow Quay, from which Gannet and Lerina used to depart for Lundy a century or more before.
AUTHOR

TABLE OF LUNDY PACKET SUCCESSION

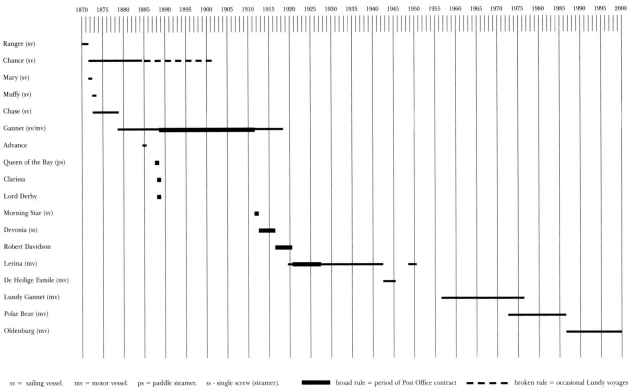

sv = sailing vessel.   mv = motor vessel.   ps = paddle steamer.   ss - single screw (steamer).   ▬▬▬ broad rule = period of Post Office contract   ▬ ▬ ▬ broken rule = occasional Lundy voyages